Hashomer Hatzair, Israel, and our Jewish Heritage

a collaborative project of former members of Hashomer Hatzair in North America

compiled and edited by:
Laura (Lilit) Schatzberg and Andi Fischhoff in 2021

Softcover ISBN: 979-8-9854014-0-0
Ebook ISBN: 979-8-9854014-1-7

Acknowledments:

Thanks go to E. Kaufman Levy (Tamar), her website is
www.starartsby Tamar.com, for permission to use her paintings on page
5 and on the cover and her dino cartoon on page 4.

Thanks also to Dorothea Dorenz, Shellie Sherman and Tzippy Kleiner
for allowing us to reproduce their artwork.

Thank you to all the people who sent in photos to use and to Susie
Browar for the photos of her mother's quilts.

And of course, thanks to all those who so generously shared their
stories, without which there would be no book.

The editors accept full responsibility for any and all technical errors but
none for the content of the material. That is the writers' alone.

Hashomer Hatzair, Israel and Our Jewish Heritage

Table of Contents

By Way of Introduction

We all met as pre-teens or teens in a socialist-Zionist youth movement called Hashomer Hatzair (The Young Guard). That was a long time ago. We are now in our 70s. Those shared experiences during our formative years cemented a bond between us that has survived our going on our separate paths. Over the intervening years there have been reunions, both official and spontaneous. Some of us have remained close friends and others haven't been in contact for 50 years.

Several years ago, in 2005, Eydie/Tamar began sending out whimsical holiday greetings to us 'dinosaurs' via email. Every Jewish holiday I looked forward to receiving her creative card and hearing from so many old friends.

Then came the COVID pandemic of 2020 and the zoom age with its challenges, tragedies and unexpected benefits. Maybe having more free time created a space to delve into the past. Dottee, Andi and Eric suggested using this zoom tool to have a virtual reunion where people, from the comfort of their homes, could reconnect in a way that had not been possible before. After two zoom meetings with 24 people or so at the first and more at the second, Mencher and Yehuda suggested a smaller group have a more focused discussion about HH and our Jewish identity. Here is what Mencher says about that.

"The original motivation for this avalanche of reminiscences about HH was Lewie's and my curiosity regarding the connection of our HH alumni to their Jewish heritage, in the past and in the present. We quickly realized that the friends from HH that we have spent so much time with, while in the movement and afterwards, had diverse and interesting backgrounds, of which few of us were aware, and, I suspect, were actively relegated to secondary importance by the madrichim and shlichim trying to get us to break free and become the "New Jew" on kibbutz in Israel.

Although much of the discussion has now centered around HH, my main interest remains in the evolution of our relation to Jewish heritage. I know that I have undergone a great change from cynical, dogmatic anti-religious attitudes (a la HH) to greater interest in our history and greater familiarity and comfort with the history and texts. Nothing to budge me from my atheism, but also no longer a "stranger" to the sources."

At that zoom Andi suggested we put our thoughts into a booklet and invite everyone to contribute. I volunteered to edit and produce it with Andi's help and here it is. I think it is a document that shows us as unique individuals who have remained part of an unusually long-lasting group of friends. As you read our thoughts you will see that for many of us HH became a family in the best sense of the word – one we had chosen and where we were accepted as we were.

The easiest way to present the stories was alphabetical by first name.

We have added remembrances of those of our friends who are no longer with us.

And for our readers who do not speak Hebrew, we have included a glossary. As a way of introducing members to the Hebrew language many things and activities were referred to by their Hebrew words. Our parents and siblings may have heard us talk about what we did when we went to the movement and wondered what language we were speaking. For example: Our madricha led a sicha in our kvutza about Tanach in the ken on shabbat. Which translated means – Our leader (counselor) led a discussion in our group about the bible in the meeting place on Saturday. I recently learned that this is called 'translanguaging' and is a common phenomenon among bi-linguals and polyglots.

Producing this volume has been revelatory and joyous. It has been heart-warming to hear stories we had never heard and perhaps will help us understand our friends in a new way. It has been an honor to be entrusted with the task of compiling our book. Of course, no one else volunteered! I am reminded of the vital, idealistic yet fun-loving youth we were and can see those same qualities in us as old folks.
Enjoy!
Lilit aka Laura Schatzberg
2021

Tamar/Eydie's latest Passover Greeting Dino for these times

<u>In Memoriam</u>

remembering those who have passed

Ami Isseroff

Danny Nachshen

Murray Kleiner

Naomi Schenker
Nava Mandelblatt

Pnina Isseroff
Shira Wexler

Zoie Isseroff

may their memory be a blessing

Dear A. (Andi) and L. (Lilit),

Though I enjoyed an extensive correspondence with Ami [Isseroff] during his later years, I lost those e-mail exchanges to technological mishaps and the entropic effect of quotidian obligations. I used to send Ami bags of books that traveled by ship for a month to reach him. During our few meetings in Israel, Ami and I resumed effortlessly what seemed like a lifelong, rambling, hilarious and always dazzling conversation. I shall never forget him, nor cease to miss him.

I was privileged to reconnect with Natan Yonatan, so this rare remaining message of Ami's from 2004 is doubly precious to me. Natan had just died when Ami sent it. Now there are more English translations of the poet's works.

Shabbat Shalom, and Be Well --

Love, E./ Tamar

3/12/2004 5:39 PM

Nathan's Poems.

Hi Edie,
I was appalled to discover that none of Nathan's Poems (almost) have apparently been translated into English. Is that true?
I found only two translated poems and the translations are terrible. I wonder who owns the rights (Sifriath Hapoalim I suppose).
Here they are below (after I fixed the worst and most obvious mistakes.) There is supposedly an online database of translated works, but the database is not functioning.
Cheers,
Ami

Poem by Nathan Yonathan
SONG OF THE LAND [Apparently "Shir Eretz" translated - "Song of Country"]
A country that its countrymen devours,
Of milk and honey, blue skies and flowers
It sometimes even robs
The poor man of his lamb.
A land whose gentle clods enfold,
Of salty shore end tours untold [wonder what that means]
And we its lovers - giving all
That we could give.

To Lior's friend Sephi Schaumann, who fell in the Lebanon War 1

JOSEPH HATH BEEN DEVOURED

Joseph hath been devoured, eaten by an evil beast

and what of his dreams and his children Ayelet and Ophir?

He has been devoured and is no more because God

has taken him too and left a tank charred by fire

with one torn phylactery in the turret.

If after battle there should be some place

where friends meet, look for his handsome face,

say to him. "Brother, brother, for nine years

after you on the roads, dressed in armour, I breathed

dust and love. Now I'm coming to rest

my worn out head on your shoulder."

All of us relied on him always, you used to say

after the war. So if there is such a place

tell him that we wait from day to day.

For in this place, once our land,

the islands are sinking. Ashes

and rust, and our strength

is shrinking, and near the places

where he passed we desire to die

and Time like a tank

crushes, crushes...

The poet's son was killed in a tank in the 1973 Yom Kippur War. This poem is dedicated to the son's friend, who was killed 9 years later in the Lebanon War.

Ami and Natan

Dear Friends,

My brother Ami died yesterday of cardiac arrest. He was 65 years old. Kindly join me in sharing his loss with his wife, Ruti and with his children, Asaf, Amit and Michal.

Hadar Isseroff

Eulogy for Ami Isseroff Wednesday June 29, 2011

When Ami was born with a congenital heart problem, the doctors said he would not survive, but his mother, Batia, refused to listen and through her perseverance he was able, after several operations, to have an almost normal life. She always felt that he was destined for greatness. Today, she would be very proud of him.

He fulfilled her fondest dreams in that he married a sweet and caring girl and had three exceptional children, Asaf, Amit and Michal. He will always be remembered in their hearts as a loving, if irascible husband and father. But the rest of us will remember him for his wit, intellect and unique outlook on life. We shared many adventures and their retelling always brought us much pleasure.

Early on, we in his immediate family recognized, his superior mental abilities as he excelled in his studies throughout high school and college. His memory was phenomenal. As a teenager, he played the guitar and piano and his love of music continued throughout his life. With Ami's talent for writing and oral disputation, the family thought he would choose to study law. Instead, his Zionist inclinations led him to join a kibbutz in Eretz Ysrael. There, for a time, he was happy to perform socialistically heroic tasks such as driving tractors, moving irrigation pipes, feeding pigs and cleaning out their pens. Difficult as these jobs were, it was the lack of an intellectually stimulating environment that caused him to leave the kibbutz. He couldn't believe that at the end of the workday kibbutzniks preferred to watch television rather than have a rousing discussion on some aspect of world affairs, politics or the class struggle. Hence, he embarked on a program of graduate study in psychology at the Universities of Jerusalem and Haifa. It was at the University in Jerusalem that Ami met the love of his life, Ruth. Through his long and exhausting years as a graduate student, that included many disputes with his faculty advisors as well as exasperating turf wars between them, it was Ruth's love and support that kept him from giving up and returning to the States. When the warring parties and their various factions finally agreed to award him a Doctorate in Experimental Psychology we thought that he would be offered secure employment. However, the weak economy and an excess of trained psychologists made it difficult for Ami to find and keep a university job despite post-doctoral training at Yale and Worcester Universities. Fortunately, in the course of his graduate studies he had developed a number of computer skills, including the ability to write complex programs that were at the cutting edge of technology. He was able to use these skills to earn a living and to pursue a new vocation as a respected observer and opinion maker in the world's media and on the Internet. It was here that he found his true calling as an outspoken advocate for peace and good will between Palestinians and Israelis. I know that Ami believed that if ever these two peoples should arrive at a state of mutual trust and respect his major life-effort would not be in vain.

With sadness and love to you all,
Hadar Isseroff

From Mimi Gloger-Tanaman
Ami Isseroff
Ami was a character. Extremely smart and sharp-witted – and many can attest to having felt that sharpness. He was physically small, due to a heart condition that made him the first child to have open heart surgery in NY, followed by his undergoing a series of other heart surgeries. But in character, he was big! He wrote articles, and appeared in plays in HH. He made aliya and studied psychology at Hebrew University, became a lecturer, and married a fellow psychology student who was nearly twice his height, which to the bigness of character of both of them, didn't seem to matter. Ami and Ruti had two sons and a daughter, and lived in Rehovot, until his heart finally wore out. יהי זכרו ברוך

Danny

The hole in my heart, filled with your absence.

Danny Nachshen z"l was my cousin, closest friend, soul brother and muse. Below are lines from a memorial piece I wrote some years after his passing. ***Philip Clement***

One moonless, star-filled night, when we were barely sixteen, Danny asked me to come with him out to a field far from any visible lights. This was at the chava past the swimming pool. He had an astronomy chart, candle and matches and we spent two timeless hours hunched over the chart, blowing out the candle then lying on our backs trying to find the constellations. It was invariably Danny who located in the skies what the chart promised. My cousin could find his way in the darkness.

When we were ten, we volunteered to be part of the Moshava swim across Lake Otty. His best stroke at the time was an unimpressive dog paddle, and I, presumptuously, cautioned him that he may not be up for the distance. He scoffed and guffawed and confidently dog paddled — with not the slightest notion of self-doubt — across the lake and back, and beat me to the shore. From our early teens until our very last conversations when he called to tell me the bad news, we discussed and debated God, the meaning of life, quantum physics, sex, death, love, mathematics, the strongest glues, and everything in between. He told me he wrote poetry. I was embarrassed to admit I didn't understand its significance. Why would anyone write poetry? But he said it with such matter-of-factness I knew it was one more insight he was gifting me.

Shortly after his Bar Mitzvah he stopped coming around. My mother told me he was sick "but not in a physical way". There was no end to my questions but, other than deep concern, my mother had few answers. A month seemed like a year and one Friday night, when he finally walked into the Ken with a shy smile, I FLEW across the room to greet him, screaming his name. We were soul brothers from that moment onward. He introduced me to patterns in the night skies and what happens when patterns fall apart, and how poetry can describe both.

Danny was an unlikely daredevil, and didn't look the part. His genuine courage was in contrast to his pensive demeanor. He knew where he stood and took his principles seriously. One Friday night, after a peula at the ken, a car driven by 'rednecks' cut us off and forced us up against the sidewalk menacingly taunting: "Long noses! Kikes!" They dared us to get out of the car and Danny was the first to move. I grabbed the door handle desperately, "Danny, they have a baseball bat in the front seat!" I pleaded, terrified of those hooligans. "We have to, Philip, they called us long noses."

When we were nine our Madrich at Mosh dubbed him The Professor. His destiny was to be a scholar and scientist which he became and excelled at. He was fluent in

Hebrew, Yiddish and French and planned to learn German. He taught us how to suck the nectar out of certain plants, play backgammon, eat artichokes, make avocados tasty and write limericks. He and I wrote several musicals together for Mosh. Our skills didn't match Stuie's but there are a couple of our songs they still sing at Perth.

One of our rituals was going for long jogs together whether Gal On, Lahav, Eilat, Jerusalem, St. Louis, Vancouver, Tel Aviv or Montreal. The Tuesday he took his last breath I went for a long run searching the night skies for my cousin. I was an ant on an emotional volcano, my world in chaos. I was a confused thirteen year old wondering what on earth happened to my buddy, but the sky was painful and bewildering that night, my questions never more futile.

It has taken me decades to integrate his loss. I think of him and miss him terribly, but my treasure chest of memories has become more accessible, as has my appreciation of how blessed my time with him was.   יהי זכרו ברוך

p.s. Hey Nachshen! If you're reading this somewhere – Chazak!

Laura/Lilit – with a memory of Danny – 2021

I didn't know Danny all that well but we were both on seminar in 1965. In December our group joined the 12th graders from GalOn on the Tiyul Chanuka – the three-day hike in the Negev. It became a badge of honor for us, especially the girls, to be able to do the entire hike and I was determined not to fail. But after the first day my feet were a mass of blisters due to my socks buckling up and chafing toes and heels. I tended them as well as I could but was barely able to walk that second morning. And up steps Danny, stretching out his hand to me and giving encouraging words. If it hadn't been for his kindness I never would have made it through the deep wadi gravel that morning. He practically dragged me for hours, never losing faith in me when I was about to lose it myself. I have never forgotten him and was deeply sad when I heard of his passing at such a young age. Chazak indeed Danny!

Warren and Dr. Danny

The following poem was in the 1966 Camp Shomria "iton" It was written by Danny Nachshen (1947 – 1986)

LAUGHTER

Golden rays

Tossed to a singing sparrow

Down in a blackened cloud.

I close my eyes and laugh at the world,

The long, hard laugh of despair.

Yesterday the starry sky

Sang a hymn of praise to life.

Today I stand on the weary mountain,

Clinging to summer's hot spell;

Trying to erase the years of youth.

Belief was yesterday ---

Tomorrow is truth.

Danny Nachshen
Ken Gilboa – Montreal

Danny being borne to the crypt at
Beit Shaarim – Seminar 1965

Murray Kleiner Z"L

Murray was more of a brother to me than my brother. I met him at Stuyvesant High School. Both of us (together with Mencher and Yechiel) took the subway from Brooklyn to the lower East Side to get to Stuyvesant. We would walk together to Union Square to catch the subway back. Stuyvesant was a public all-boys school at the time. It was the early 1960s and the student body was in the throes of the youth rebellion against the establishment.

Murray was always full of quirky, rebellious ideas. When I met him, he was enamored with science-fiction and had the idea of large mechanical wombs where people might withdraw from life and live in semi-hibernation, with all their physical needs cared for. He had a stamp made up saying "Back to the Womb" and stamped it on desks and walls throughout the school. Murray came to me with many political ideas that were new to me. I first read the Port Huron Statement of SDS when Murray brought me a copy. I thought that he was the most interesting and intellectual person that I had ever met.

I later found out that Murray was born in a DP Camp in Germany, in fact the same one that I lived in for the first years of my life. I was born in Poland in June 1946, and then my parents fled with me to Germany. Murray's parents also fled to Germany at the same time, but he was born in September when they were already at the camp. My parents and Murray's parents knew of each other and had common acquaintances.

Mencher convinced Murray to come to Mosh Choref one winter. Murray told me that he was going to convince the Movement to abandon Zionism. When I next saw him, two weeks later, he had become a fervent Zionist. I found this conversion odd, and it was not until much later that I realized that Tzippy Linder was responsible for the conversion.

Murray and I attended Brooklyn College together for the first year. Every day, we would meet for lunch by the goldfish pond on campus and have long, involved, political, and philosophical discussions. I would know that I had won the debate when Murray would end the discussion by saying, "You're entitled to your stupid opinion!" Although I would regularly discuss my family and my difficult relations with them at the time, Murray was always closed about personal issues. I never heard him speak about his parents, his sister, or even his relations with Tzippy. During the time that we were students at Brooklyn College, Murray's parents got divorced. I heard about the divorce from my mother, who heard about it from friends. He had never mentioned it.

Murray and Tzippy moved to Israel, at first to Kibbutz Barkai. I joined them on the kibbutz in June 1967, when I came as a volunteer during the Six Day War. Later, I moved to Jerusalem to begin my medical studies and the Kleiners moved to Jerusalem. Tzippy gave birth to Mira, a beautiful and vivacious child, who gave them no end of grief. Murray got a degree in psychology, and later got a position in the Jerusalem police as a polygraph (lie detector) examiner. He enjoyed the work and helped develop polygraphy into an academic field. He was the editor of the first textbook in polygraphy.

Murray and Tzippy bought an abandoned ruin of an Arab house in an old neighborhood in Jerusalem and turned it into a beautiful and comfortable space to live in, surrounded by a wonderful garden. The house was always full of people and art and music. Friends of the Kleiner children felt comfortable in their house and would often visit, even if the children were not home. Tzippy taught art to children, both at home and at the Israel Museum. There were always interesting friends and good conversations to be had about art, history, politics, philosophy and science, at the Kleiner home. There was always a standing invitation to eat and drink as well.

After Dalia and I moved back to the United States and would return to visit Israel, the Kleiner home was our home in Israel. Murray and I would take long walks in the evening, having long discussions, and sometimes debates, about every topic in the universe. Murray remained mostly closed about personal issues but would, every once in a while, open up about both his pride in and his concerns about his children. When my children visited Israel, they also felt most comfortable and at home in the Kleiner home. When Murray died, my daughter, Avishag, said, "He was the nicest and best looking among your friends!" I miss him terribly.

May his memory be blessed ! יהי זכרו ברוך

Yehuda Reisman
Jerusalem

Murray, painted by his wife Tzippy Kleiner. Naturally, she writes about Murray in her piece.

Remembering Naomi Schenker   (1946-2020)

Naomi was born on June 25, 1946, a baby boomer. I was playing outside with the caterpillars on Linden Blvd. in Brooklyn when my parents told me there was a new addition to the family. She was an RH baby, and contracted a case of jaundice in infancy which led to 70% hearing loss, which was only identified when she was five years old.

Despite wearing a hearing aid, she always enjoyed music. Her favorite song was "This Little Light of Mine", and her favorite singer was...Ricky Nelson. Naomi identified with the fact that singer Johnny Ray also wore a hearing aid, and in her pre-movement summer camp days once appeared as a character in Gilbert and Sullivan's "Mikado". And she learned to play the autoharp, an instrument that was played by the Carter Family and also John Sebastian of "The Lovin' Spoonful". She was also fascinated by the history of American presidents, and knew the names of all of them in order of their presidency!

Naomi became an active member of Hashomer Hatzair, Ken Massada, and went regularly to the Moshava summer camp, which she thoroughly enjoyed.

In 1965 she spent half a year on a seminar on Kibbutz Mishmar Haemek and Kibbutz Galon. Joey Beinin told me he shared a room with her and two other girls, and there is at least one photo of her with the entire group.

In 1968 she came on aliya by boat (no one took planes at the time), and I remember meeting her in Haifa together with Aunt Rose, our mother's older sister, an adventurous travel agent who arranged to be in Israel when she arrived.

Between 1968 and 1970 she was on Kibbutz Galon with her *garin*, and particularly enjoyed her time working in the chicken coops. Unfortunately, when her candidacy for membership came up, the *sichat kibbutz* conditioned her membership on the family paying half of any medical expenses that might appear in the future, with the kibbutz members split between the veteran Polish founders who wanted the condition while the veteran American members disagreed and said she should be an unconditional member. Naomi was insulted by this response, and in 1970 she moved to Jerusalem, as did many other members of her *garin* who were also frustrated with elements of life on Galon.

Naomi was proud of her independence, and worked for 27 years in a responsible position in the Israel Postal Authority. Her work there gave her meaning and structure, and also a social framework.

Naomi also loved to travel, visiting friends from abroad she had made on the kibbutz, relatives, and exotic landscapes.

When she moved to Jerusalem, she lived at first on picturesque Al Harizi Street in the center of the city. Our father used to stay in her apartment a few times a week when he was working at the Jewish Agency for Israel, which was just two blocks away on King George Street.

In 1991 she moved to Emek Refaim in the German Colony neighborhood established by the Templars in the 19th century, near the old train station which is now The First Station entertainment complex.

When I began working in Jerusalem at the Palestine-Israel Journal in 2002, I used to stay over a few times a week, and she always offered to cook a high cholesterol dinner which today I would try to avoid, but then enjoyed.

Friends who lived in the neighborhood, like Tzippy Kleiner – her husband Murray was in Naomi's *kvutza* back in Brooklyn – told me that every encounter with her on the street was filled with warm, positive vibes.

She went to ceramics classes, loved to make things to fire in a kiln, and also had a big collection of dolls from everywhere. She read a lot, and enjoyed seeing movies that our mother would recommend to her by fax every week.

One thing I always associated with her was her love of cats. She had a series of cats, beginning in Brooklyn, and continuing in Jerusalem, and they almost all had the same name – Fluffy. The last one lived to the ripe old age of 22!

Naomi struggled against all obstacles to maintain her independence, something that all of us admired tremendously. She always enjoyed extended family gatherings as well.

Unfortunately, about 15 years ago, the Postal Authority had to make budget cuts, and they forced all the workers over 55 to take early retirement, while providing them with a good pension. The loss of her work environment and structure was problematic, and her hearing problems also began to affect her mobility. It became difficult for her to continue living independently, and after a few care givers, it became clear that the best solution for her was to go to a nursing home. For four years she was in a nursing home in Ramat Gan, and during the last four years in Bnei Brak. One of the things that gave her great satisfaction there was to continue to draw and paint. The staff at the different nursing homes always appreciated how respectful and polite she was to them.

In recent years, whenever I would visit her and ask if she wanted anything, besides the diet coke that I would always bring, she said no need, because she hoped to return home to Jerusalem the following week. She also dreamed of a boyfriend who would one day share her life.

Despite the fact that the nursing home was in Bnei Brak, which was hard hit by Covid-19, her nursing home had no cases of the virus. After three months, external visits by one family member were allowed once again, but my planned visit was not to be.

I will always remember her, and apologize for once throwing a hamburger at her when we were very young, and also for the fact that I never allowed her to beat me in ping pong, only to come close. It's hard to lose your only sister.

Her tombstone says:

אחות, בת דודה ודודה יקרה,

האומץ, הנחשיות והאופטימיות שלך היו השראה לכולנו

זכרך ישאר בליבינו תמיד

Beloved sister, cousin, and aunt, your courage, determination, and optimism were an inspiration to all of us. Your memory will remain in our hearts forever.

Hillel

Naomi is on the far right next to Chaya Strumpf, Pnina Braff, and Aviva Weiss

Nava (Ellen) Mandelblatt (1945-1977)

Like a number of others from that period in the movement, Nava's parents were members of the Communist Party. Her father, Sol, even served in the Lincoln Brigade in the Spanish Civil War, though he went on to abandon the family when she was nine, a rare occurrence in that period. She grew up in the left-wing environment of the Amalgamated Cooperative Housing Project in The Bronx next to Van Courtlandt Park, and spent a few summers at Camp Kinderland, which an article on *Tablet* describes as follows:

Camp Kinderland was founded in 1923 as a respite for children who were living in New York City's tenements. Its founders were mostly immigrants—factory workers, tailors, Yiddish teachers, union organizers—who put their houses up for mortgage and bought the camp. These were the "weird Jews," longtime staffer Judee Rosenbaum explains in the film, socialist Jews who didn't keep kosher or have bar mitzvahs but who had deep ties to the anti-czarist movements back home and the labor and anti-racist movements in the United States. And even though they weren't religious, Rosenbaum says, they connected their Jewishness with a sense of social justice.

Ellen eventually discovered Hashomer Hatzair, Ken Hachoresh and *moshava* as an alternative to Kinderland, and that's when she became Nava. That's also when I discovered her. I asked her out for our first date when we were on a night-time movement voyage to the exotic fifth NYC borough on the Staten Island Ferry.

We moved to Kibbutz Barkai in the Fall of 1963, and on Friday night November 22nd, sang at a local talent evening the first performance of "Blowing in the Wind" in Israel, the day that President Kennedy was assassinated.

Although she hadn't studied Hebrew before, she worked very hard to become fluent in the language so that she would be able to speak to our child, after she was born, in Hebrew as a "mother tongue".

There's an interesting anecdote about our daughter's name, Rama. There used to be a Saturday night city-wide movement cultural/political evening in Manhattan, I think at the headquarters of the progressive District 65 union where Elana Michaelson's father, Bill, was one of the vice presidents, and one of the evenings was devoted to Irma Lindheim and her autobiographical book "Parallel Quest". Lindheim had been the second president of Hadassah, and after becoming close to the movement, moved to Kibbutz Mishmar Haemek in 1933 at the age of 47. Over the years, she had divided her time between Israel and the States, and also ran for Congress on the American Labor Party ticket while supporting Henry Wallace's Progressive Party candidacy for president in 1948. Nava and I wrote and sang a song in her honor at the event. Since Irma's Hebrew name was Rama, when she heard that our daughter's name was Rama, she thought the name was in her honor. Not quite.

We had simply gone through a book of suggested Hebrew names for children, and in those days, when you didn't know the sex of the child in advance, had decided that if it was a girl we liked the name Rama, and if a boy, Ram.

Having been a graduate of Music and Art High School, Nava was multi-talented in the arts, music, sculpture, painting and of course dance, having studied with a teacher who had been taught by Martha Graham. When Yehudit Arnon of Kibbutz Ga'aton decided to found an inter-kibbutz modern dance troupe in 1970, she looked for kibbutz members who had training in dance. Nava was a natural candidate for the troupe, and was the lead female dancer in the first shows of the Kibbutz Contemporary Dance Company.

In 1977, while rehearsing for the traditional *Had Gadya* dance performance for the Pesach seder on Kibbutz Barkai, she fainted due to an aneurysm. She sadly passed away soon afterwards.

Our daughter Rama now lives in the Amalgamated Housing Project where Nava originally grew up. An interesting post-script has to do with her son's name, Evan. When he was born, his father, an Italian-American, named Rocco Jr. (his father was also Rocco), wanted to name him Rocco the 3rd. Rama couldn't imagine having a son with such a name, so the solution was to call him Evan, which of course means rock in Hebrew, and is also a tribute to Nava's original English name Ellen.

Hillel Schenker

Mimi Tanaman's Memories of Pnina Isseroff ז"ל

I was happy to make Pnina, Zoie's blond, blue-eyed little sister, my sister too. I remember one Moshava when we braided our hair together, her long blond hair and my long black hair, into one multi-colored braid and walked around thus attached for hours. Pnina loved to laugh, and this characteristic was part of her all her life. She loved to pun, and I recall particularly on tiyulim, she kept everyone entertained with her punning (I think they were called "stinky pinkies"??). And she loved to sing. We were both in Tzfira's choir. Her default persona was a gush of enthusiasm, making her fun to be around.

Pnina made aliya with her family in 1965 (I think she was 15) and managed to get through high school in Hebrew, after which she studied music and choir conducting both at Rubin Academy in Jerusalem and for a time abroad, avoiding the IDF (Israel Defense Forces).

Pnina had studied piano as a child, and music flowed from her. Any instrument she picked up would soon be producing lovely sounds. When the string band Zoie and I were in needed a new guitarist, Pnina practiced a bit and was ready to go, joining us in performances around the country playing guitar and singing.

Suzie Kleiner, Murray's sister, was Pnina's lifelong best friend. They shared an apartment in Jerusalem, and maintained contact even after Suzie moved abroad.

Pnina married Alan Levin, a South African oleh, and they had two sons; Ariel, who started life blond like his mom, and Elad, a gingey like his Uncle Zoie. In our adult years, Pnina and I, with our respective families, shared a two-family home in Ra'anana.

If I were to try and point out a problem Pnina had, I would say her problem was that she was too talented. After studying music and choir conducting, she had a brief brush with being an orchestra conductor (when she was in a relationship with famous conductor, Lucas Foss, and friends with Zubin Mehta). She composed music and had a huge library of beautiful songs and full musicals that she had written. She also wrote poetry, essays and plays. She tried her hand at graphic art, conducted choirs, taught piano, taught voice, performed solo as a singer, performed in community theatre productions, did Qi Gong, and gave very successful workshops to patients of Parkinson's disease. As she said once in a one-woman play she wrote and performed, "Who shall I be today?"

Pnina passed away, far too young, from cancer. She managed to publish a book of poems and essays, "Magical Machine", shortly before departing this world. As it says on the book jacket, "Isseroff has been writing poetry since childhood, always thinking she'll 'do something about it some day'. In recent years, following divorce and a diagnosis of cancer, she realized that 'some day' is now." The book reflects Pnina's love of life, her children, her creativity, and her attempts to make sense of and cope with the disease. **יהי זכרה ברוך**

Remembering Shira – Joan (Nechama) Rahav

Shira Wexler was my best friend, until I left for Israel when I was 15. I first met Shira when we were both 11. We had both just joined the Ken in the Bronx. We cloned together, from our first meeting onward, and became inseparable. It was the first utter intimacy I ever had. We lived and breathed each other's lives. We eventually went to the same high school. We would meet halfway there, and travel together. After school we were still together. When I eventually got home, I got on the phone with her, and we talked and talked all evening. I was in her house all the time. She was in my house all the time. She knew everything about me. I knew everything about her. We shared everything. It was the most complete immersion in another person's life that I have ever had. Since I was young and naive and had never left home, this was a primary, pure and innocent connection. We were complete best friends - at school, at camp, in the movement. We didn't look exactly the same but we had the same hair, and people thought we were twins. One day at Bronx Science, someone came over to Shira and asked her, "How come you are so much more beautiful than your twin?" We were both, at that time, beautiful but God bless her, she had the face of Helen of Troy, a face to sink a thousand ships. She was so very beautiful.

This kind of love was not called love back then. Girls, to remind you, didn't really matter. It was boys, that one was supposed to strive to get. Indeed, I had a wonderful boyfriend, she had a wonderful boyfriend, and there were other close friends in our "pod" (Amira Levine, Shuly Dubinsky, Phil Treisman, Teddy Vermont, Gedalia Granoff, and others). Many years later, I read an article in Ms. Magazine by Gloria Steinem, which pointed out that women never gave weight to the love they had for other women, only to love for men. It hit me at that time like a ton of bricks, that I had really loved Shira infinitely. I just didn't have a frame of reference or a vocabulary for it.

Looking back, for the four years that we were together, my love for her was indeed infinite. Then I left New York and went to Israel, and it was all over. Mind you, I had no phone, no air mail letter allotments, no way of sharing where I was and what was happening. I was terribly traumatized by the move to Israel. It was essentially a re-enactment of earlier traumas, and who back then knew the word trauma, or the tools to process it? I changed completely. Out of necessity (I thought), I became a whole new person. I tried to speak Hebrew without an accent; I gave up my way of thinking, my way of being (at least I pretended so to myself). I was exposed to a whole new life and I needed to try and survive. I indeed learned to speak Hebrew without an accent. I learned how to act as if I was a native Israeli. On the occasions when I went back to New York and called Shira, and she came to see me, our lives had evolved. She was different, I was different, and the lives that we had shared with each other had morphed. Sure, I still cared for her a lot, but it was never the same again.

After I married, she moved to Las Vegas, and I lost touch with her. I didn't see her for many years. One bright day, it must've been about 1997, she called me out of the blue. She was living in Starrett City in Brooklyn with her father. She had escaped from her husband in Las Vegas and moved in with her father. I told her, "I'll come visit your father". She said "no no no". He at that time was senile. She didn't want me to see him that way. We set up a routine where she began to come and visit me in Manhattan. She was not well; she was terribly heavy and sick. She was unrecognizable. She was involved in a lawsuit that was supposed to be settled and bring a lot of money to her. The intimacy we had once had was gone. I struggled to bring up the memory of it. I had affection for her still, but she was not the person I once knew. She had lived a different life from me. Her reality was different, her priorities were different. We continued to meet. I tried to share with her something of what was going on in my life, but I did get the impression that she didn't understand what I was trying to share. Her lawsuit eventually resolved and she did get a settlement of money. With that money she moved to Phoenix, Arizona and once again she was out of my life. She called me from Arizona a while later. It seems she had been living with her son and her son's wife, but at a certain moment her son and her daughter-in-law got divorced and the new girlfriend moved in and made life difficult for her. She told me about it and said she might move back to New York. The next I heard, she had died.

After she died I experienced the most heart rending shock. She had become so far away and so different, I hadn't thought my heart would be broken. When she was gone, the love of many years ago come flooding back. I became paralyzed with the thought of what I had lost. I do remember that pure and tender girlfriend to girlfriend love with endless tenderness. I miss my twin and my love desperately. Rest in peace beautiful beautiful Shira. May your memory be for a blessing.

Nechama (Joan)

From Shuli
Shira

I first met Shira, Carol Wexler, at moshava in 1960. My third mosh, her first. I remember her as one of the most beautiful girls I knew, and was just so jealous of that long blond hair!! I vividly remember her laugh and her friendship, that survival day where we ended up at some borsht belt hotel and arranged for us all to perform. I don't remember what the rest of the group did. Shira and I sang, literally for our supper! We sang the songs we loved to harmonize in both English and Hebrew. We always loved singing together. During the school year she attended Bronx Science with I believe Nechama and Dov G. She was also a very accomplished sketch artist, but unfortunately never pursued that possibility. We spoke daily on the phone, as teenagers do, discussing boys and making new harmonies for many songs.

Unfortunately I lost contact with her for many years. She had her share of bad luck and bad marriages and then a terrible car crash which left her badly crippled. We got in touch with each other again because her son stumbled onto something she had with my name on it. Unfortunately, she passed away about a year after that. I believe that Amira was in touch with her some of the time when I was not, so maybe she has something to add.

Remembering Zoie Isseroff

From David Mencher

I can't say that I knew Zoie well, although he certainly counted among my friends. I really enjoyed playing music with him, and was grateful for his (and Noam and Laya's) welcoming me into their home and inner circle, but my relationship with Zoie never included the introspection that factors so strongly in the deep friendships that I have made over the years.

A snippet of memory – upon arriving in Israel in October 1968, Lewie met me at the airport with his Vespa, and we proceeded to Jerusalem, where I stayed for a few days before being called to show up in Gal On. I remember being shuttled around by Zoie in his Mini station wagon, and being treated to a delicious dinner at the Golden Chicken Restaurant in East Jerusalem by Noam and Laya. Life seemed so rich and exciting back then.

Perhaps I could have tried harder to get to know Zoie – I don't know. In the last ten years or so, despite our shared experiences of previous years, political and social "issues" often made visits tense, and I am sorry for that.

From Mimi Tanaman nee Gloger

Introduction
From the age of about 17, I was part of the Isseroff family, and remained so until my divorce from Zoie after a 17-year marriage plus two daughters, Lisa and Tali. I think I was happy to marry the family as much as to marry Zoie. So I will start with his parents.

Noam and Laya were a fairy tale couple who married for love, against much advice to the contrary, and maintained a loving relationship throughout their lives. Noam was handsome, charming and fun. Laya was beautiful, kind and caring. And I loved them both. They had both been members of Hashomer in their youth, and as adults, were members of the affiliated API, Americans for a Progressive Israel. They were also a regular feature at the Shomria summer camps, to be near their little girl who was quite attached to them. In the 50s the family, Noam and Laya with a young Zoie and Pnina, went to spend a year in Israel. Noam was actually born in Jerusalem, and so was his mother. His father arrived in Jerusalem in his youth with the ke'hilah from their Russian town. Noam's father was a rebel who was thrown out of yeshiva for reading A.D. Gordon. He worked in Degania, Israel's first kibbutz. He and his bride lived in Damascus for a time where Noam's brother – Ami Isseroff's father – was born, and where Noam's mother ran the city's first Hebrew kindergarten. They eventually moved to New York where Noam's father became head of the Hebrew Teachers Union. They always intended to return to Israel and finally did, some 40 years later.

It had also always been Noam and Laya's intention to make aliya. In the 60s Noam was instrumental in organizing a group of families full of idealism and ready to make aliya together, set up an industry, and build a community. As often happens when ideals meet reality, it didn't all turn out as they would have liked and many of the families returned to the US, although a few managed to stay. Their aliya prompted my marriage to Zoie.

Zoie Isseroff Z'L

He was a leader in HH, a "macher", looked up to and respected, which was for me part of the original attraction. The plan was, I would study psychology, he would study sociology, and we would write erudite journal articles together. The reality was, after changing majors every year, he finally stopped studying. However, he was not without a range of talents. He was an impressive guitarist, and taught himself to be even more impressive on the mandolin. He also taught himself to play fiddle and autoharp. He was a reasonable chess player and an excellent photographer. He worked in a photo lab for a time and turned our bathroom at home into a darkroom where he developed his own pictures (remember those?! ☺). During his university years he wrote poetry and helped produce the English Department's literary magazine. He also had an exhibition with a talented artist friend (Michael Gitlin) who incorporated Zoie's poetry into his etchings. This friend, also an accomplished classical guitarist and teacher, got Zoie into classical guitar as well, and again, Zoie became proficient at it and became a teacher of classical guitar. During our string band years he proved to be a likable and funny character on stage.

He remarried (to Reida) after our divorce and had another daughter, Gillie. For many years he and our younger daughter, Tali, attended yoga classes together once a week. After moving to Kfar Yona, he began doing Krav Magen, becoming very involved and accomplished. The entire class and teacher attended his funeral and posthumously presented his earned black belt. His passing was sudden, the only consolation of which is that he did not suffer. **יהי זכרו ברוך**

Zoie Isseroff Z'L

When I met Zoie, we were 12 years old and he was a wild, out of control kid with bright orange hair. Soon after I arrived at the ken, he ran into a wall, carrying a girl on his shoulders. As I remember it, there was some damage to the wall, but not to Zoie or to the girl. He was expelled from the ken for several weeks, but he could not be expelled permanently, because his parents were HH aristocracy. I also remember that he would come over to me occasionally and punch me in the shoulder and then run away. I was very annoyed by this, but he was much quicker than I was. This continued until one day I was ready for him and hit him back hard and he decided to stop doing that.

I remember the summer in Moshava immediately after my Bar Mitzvah. Our group was in two large tents combined. Zoie was the leader of the group and organized all activities. One day he took me into the woods and taught me to smoke cattails wrapped in newspaper, as cigarettes. It was not at all tasty but did seem very cool!

I left the movement at the age of 13 and then returned at the age of 16. By this time, Zoie was less wild but very much a central person in the movement. I was especially impressed by his musical abilities. I had grown up in a home essentially without music. I also had no musical talent. Zoie and several others in our group had musical talent and there was constant music in the movement.

Zoie and I became madrichim and we would often spend Saturdays together with our chanichim. We would then come back to my house after the peula, take a nap, eat dinner, and then go to spend the evening at an activity with our own age group. I never heard him speak of school, or of career choice, or of demands from his parents. He once, years later, said to me that his parents could not agree on how to raise him, and decided not to.

Zoie was a bright, charming, talented, charismatic young man. The girls loved him, and the boys wanted to emulate him. He married at 19, and then moved to Israel with Mimi. I, at the time, thought that he was the coolest guy in the world. I could only rarely find a girl to go out with, and Zoie was married.

In January 1968, I moved to Jerusalem and started to study medicine at Hadassah Medical School. I was alone in a foreign country and had trouble speaking Hebrew. The friends that I had were far away on Kibbutz Galon. Zoie and Mimi took me in, introduced me to their large group of interesting friends, and invited me to their many parties. Zoie helped me find a room to live in, and then, each time that I had to move, he came with his small Mini-Minor station wagon to move the two trunks that contained all of my possessions.

When I was a student in Jerusalem, I frequently ran out of money at the end of the month and was left eating spaghetti and vanilla wafers. Sometimes I would resort to subterfuge. I would drop in at Mimi and Zoie's apartment at about 5 PM. Sometime later, they would be about to sit down to dinner and would invite me to join them. I would feign reluctance and make them ask me several times before eating their food.

Zoie and Mimi decided to try their hand as professional musicians and formed a country and western string band called "The Golden City String Band" together with Sid and Hadassah Singer, an English couple. I would go to many of their performances, and rehearsals.

I would occasionally bring girls to their performances, in an attempt to improve my standing by association. When I started to go out with Dalia, I, of course, brought her to meet Zoie and Mimi, and took her to performances of the 'Golden City'. When we got married, the Golden City String Band provided the music at our wedding. Among their songs, was a Hebrew version of "Roll Out the Barrel" written by Dalia. March 5, our wedding day was the same day that Zoie and Mimi got married and for years afterwards, we would celebrate our anniversaries together. When Lisa, their first child was born, I was there with a bottle of whiskey and when Avishag, our first child was born, Zoie was there to support me with a bottle of whiskey.

I moved back to the US, and although I came back to Israel to visit frequently, we slowly lost our close ties, especially after Zoie and Mimi got divorced. Today, I terribly miss Zoie, but what I miss the most, was the young vibrant carrot-headed Zoie that is still so vivid in my memories.

יהי זכרו ברוך

Yehuda Reisman
Jerusalem

Our Stories

Amira Levine / Marilyn Suffet

I spent my first five years in a fairly religious, Yiddish-speaking, immigrant environment. We lived over my grandparents' little grocery store on the corner of Sutter Avenue and Strauss Street in Brooklyn. I was too young to be aware of being Jewish or of having any identity. In 1951, when I was five, my father finished school and we moved to Babylon, Long Island. It was a big culture shock for me with only a few Jewish families in our small town. The main Jewish identity was religious, although my parents were moving away from their European roots. As I grew older, I rebelled against religion, especially as I realized how misogynistic it was – all religions, not just Judaism. But still I dutifully went to Friday night and Saturday services, Sunday school, and Hebrew school two days a week after regular school. That was the only way at that point in my life to have a Jewish identity. I never experienced outright antisemitism but was always acutely aware that I did not quite fit in.

In the summer of 1959, at age twelve and at the Babylon Town Pool and Beach, I was finally old enough to hang out with the "big" kids at the juke box and not with the mothers and children. In 1960, my uncle, who had been in Hashomer Hatzair as a young man – some of you might remember his son, my cousin Neal Farber and Neil's wife Varda – convinced my parents to send me to a camp so I could learn some Hebrew songs. I did not want to go. I had planned on spending my summer, as I did the year before, at the pool. I was very angry and ready to hate camp. Shomria turned out to be the best thing that happened to me. I met Nechama, Shira, Shuly, and everyone else, and I was hooked. My life now had definition and purpose far beyond the typical suburban culture that I was becoming a part of.

I did not always agree with the politics of HH. I was developing a more anarchistic world view and didn't agree with concepts such as democratic centralism. But I don't think the purpose of this project is to have a detailed political discussion. Anyway, for me that wasn't the important part of HH. It was the comradeship and the belonging to something of importance.

I was very disappointed with kibbutz life when I went on seminar on Kibbutz Dalya in 1964-1965 and when I spent three months on Galon in 1967. It reminded me of life in suburbia. I didn't like how they were raising their children and the second class status of most women. Still, I remained in HH and thought I would eventually live on kibbutz.

I left HH in the summer of 1968 after a very contentious meeting at the chava, which I walked out of very angry. It was still important to me to be politically involved, and soon after I met Stephen at a meeting of Resistance, an anti-draft organization. We have been together ever since, got married in 1969, and had a daughter in 1970.

We have been active in many organizations over the years, including Resistance, War Resistance League, Jewish Socialist Community, New American Movement, and Occupy Wall Street. We lived in the Resistance Commune in Brooklyn in 1968-1969. I wasn't quite ready to give up on communal living. We are now more involved with the musical aspects of activism through People's Music Network and Peoples' Voice Café. I'm still hanging out at the Oasis singing.

We are both retired now. I was a nurse and then a midwife. Stephen was a teacher and then a special education supervisor. Our daughter is a principal at an alternative high school. We still live in New York City and plan to remain here. Although our ties to Judaism are strictly secular, we are proud to be members of the Tribe.

Despite some very serious political differences, I am grateful for my years in HH and for having known all of you. It has been joyous for me to reconnect.

Amira, in red shirt, with Marty Braff, Ariela, Eric and Yechiel
(Martin Felder)

Andi (Marks) Fischhoff -Pittsburgh, PA

I grew up in a household that didn't take religious observance or Jewish tradition seriously. My mother and I showed up at Passover seders hosted by our neighbors, and we attended high holiday services but no other religious services during the year. I remember an exchange with my father, who died when I was nine from cancer, when I was about seven. I sneezed and he said, "Gesundheit." I asked him, "What's that?" He explained and said, "You need to start going to Hebrew School." After my bat mitzvah, I stopped going to synagogue and I don't remember that my mother and I ever talked about it.

Meanwhile, a good friend and I were getting involved in civil rights activism. My mother, thinking that it would be good for me to go to a Jewish summer camp, found an ad for Camp Shomria in the NY Times magazine, and I went to a reunion of shomrim to see if I felt comfortable in the group. I did. I went to moshava that summer and spent the rest of my teenage years in the movement. Jewish heritage had meaning for me only through the perspective of Hashomer Hatzair during those years. Religious observance had no place in the movement, as far as I could tell, and I was firmly an atheist, but Judaism definitely informed my world view and my values.

Ironically, during the six years Baruch and I spent in kibbutz and in Jerusalem, we never attended a religious service. Disillusioned with kibbutz (I understood that "women's roles" in the kibbutz -- at least in the two kibbutzim where we lived -- consisted of traditional work in the kitchen, laundry, and childcare, rather than sharing more "productive" work with men, as we'd been led to believe), I realized, too, that our education in the movement never extended to an understanding of how Zionism affected Palestinians. When we moved to Jerusalem, we became involved in Palestinians' rights activities.

Moving to Eugene, Oregon, in 1974 with our three-year old daughter, we became involved in a chavurah, then in the local synagogue, where the rabbi was our age, and we felt very comfortable. Ironically, during those years, we also helped organize a kibbutz-like community called Shivtei Shalom not far from Eugene, which, unfortunately, lasted only a few years.

We moved to Pittsburgh in 1987 with our three children. Here, we've been involved for the last 34 years in the local Reconstructionist synagogue, Dor Hadash, and, while we rarely attend services, I've become very engaged in the social action and racial justice work going on through the synagogue. Ours was one of the three congregations attacked during the Tree of Life shooting October 27, 2018, and that led to a lot of local activism in the area of gun control and community relations. We formed an organization called Squirrel Hill (our neighborhood) Stands Against Gun Violence. It's a discouraging struggle, since gun ownership is increasing here, and seemingly everywhere else, as the country becomes more polarized politically, and right-wing extremism and antisemitism become more prevalent.

But we need to keep trying to elect legislators who are prepared to work with us on this issue.

The shooting at Tree of Life and the deaths of 11 worshippers was certainly the most horrific experience of antisemitism I've ever had. The shooter, whose trial is still not scheduled, is a local right-wing extremist whose thinking was shaped by social media and who was, in his words, especially angry at the Jews because of their support for refugees and immigrants. Our synagogue is affiliated with HIAS and our social action committee was planning a "refugee Shabbat" event that the shooter learned about online. I've wrestled with the question of my personal responsibility. Should I, and my synagogue community, stop advocating for refugees and immigrants? I don't think so. This work is central to my Jewish values. Since the shooting, I feel even more strongly that the Jewish community isn't safe unless we're all – refugees and immigrants, Blacks, Muslims, indigenous people, and Jews – safe. Social activism is even more important to me than before. I volunteer with the Bhutanese community, with an out-of-school program in a largely Black community where we're developing a Social Justice Resource Center, and with an organization led by an Orthodox rabbi that works with members of the Jewish community who are incarcerated and their families. Working with that organization is giving me more understanding of the Orthodox community than I've ever had before.

I'd say that Hashomer Hatzair definitely shaped my political thinking and attitudes toward my Jewish heritage. I'm very grateful to have been in the movement and grateful for all the friends I still treasure from that era.

Andi with Margie at the Chava

Ariela Ehrlich

I was raised in suburban Long Island in a middle-class family with aspirations much higher than their income. We lived in a bland middle-class bubble surrounded by people just like us. Jews were the smart kids and the Italians and Irish were the jocks. Our entire street was Jewish – people just like us. We knew we were Jewish. We celebrated Hanukkah with candles and presents every night. We celebrated Pesach with a big family seder, but ate bread the rest of the holiday. And a favorite Sunday breakfast was bacon and eggs.

One of my grandfathers was born in Brooklyn. He served in the Brooklyn Navy Yard during WWI. The other grandparents had come to NY as young teenagers before WWI. My Galitzianer grandfather said that he had come to America to escape religious persecution – his parents! Needless to say they were all secular, cultural, Jews. None of them were especially interested in Israel. They had lost only very distant relatives in the Holocaust.

My father had been a soldier in WWII. He fought in North Africa, Sicily, and after landing in Normandy, fought his way across Europe to the border with Germany. At that point he broke down and was sent home in March 1945. He suffered from "combat fatigue" and never really recovered. He hadn't seen the concentration camps in Germany or Poland, but he had liberated transit camps in France. He was a staunch American patriot and a Republican. My mother, as a teenager, had been a "Young Pioneer" and had volunteered in a conscientious objector camp in upstate NY. I was told to never speak of my mother's past due to my father's work as a government contractor. Her uncles and aunts were members of the Communist Party. One of her uncles was the head of the Brooklyn branch. He died speaking at the podium.

We spent the year I was in first grade in Sedalia, MO. My dad was a plumbing/ heating contractor on an air force base, and my parents sought out the tiny Jewish community. We joined a Reform synagogue that year and became friendly with the Jewish mayor's family. But I was the only Jew in my entire elementary school. And I have never forgotten being chased home in tears by a classmate's older brother who shouted at me that I had killed Christ and crying to my mother that I hadn't killed anyone.

I spent two summers, aged 10 and 11, at the University Settlement House overnight camp in Beacon, NY. I was sent there by my parents because it was cheap. They had no idea that it was a "progressive" camp run under the guiding hand of Pete Seeger! The campers were a diverse group – a mixture of children from the Settlement House's Lower East Side neighborhood – Blacks and Hispanics – and the middle-class Jewish grandchildren of the original campers! It was a life-changing experience that opened my mind and my heart. It also introduced me to folk music and protest songs - as Pete Seeger usually led our nightly sing-a-longs! My last summer at that camp my counselor lent me the book she had just finished reading, "Exodus". And that book, at the age of 11, sparked my on-going interest in Israel and the Holocaust and my Jewish heritage.

Back home, I began studying Hebrew on my own from records. I began reading every book I could find in the library about Israel and the Holocaust.

Before the summer I turned thirteen, I found an ad at the back of the NY Times Magazine for the Young Judea camp, Tel Yehuda. I learned about traditional Judaism at that camp, (we prayed on Shabbat and after meals) and also about Israel. I met my first Israelis – teenage Scouts who served as counselors. I stayed on for a second session and I attended their first "ulpan" where I first began learning spoken Hebrew. I found an old book in the camp library about a group of teenagers from Habonim Baltimore who had made aliyah to Kibbutz Kfar HaNasi before 1948. Their description of life as pioneers on a kibbutz gave me the idea that I could do that too.

The following winter, on the F train on my way home from the Israeli Dance Concert at Carnegie Hall, I noticed a group of teens in blue shirts and white strings. I approached them, asking them if they were in Habonim (the book I had read in the summer described blue shirts with red strings – but I wasn't sure.) Their answer was no! We are in Hashomer Hatzair! Amos Ben Yisrael, the shaliach at the time, was with them and he invited me to come to the Queens ken on Friday night and arranged for me to come to the city by train with an older girl named Nava who lived in a Long Island town close to mine. She brought me to the ken – where I was warmly welcomed by my kvutza – Tamar, Mimi, Andi, Dottee, Laurie, Shuli, Eric, and others. I had finally found a group of kids my age with whom I felt I belonged. I found friends who embraced me and accepted me. We had fun – we danced, we sang, we went on adventures around the city, we were silly and laughed, we learned about Israel, Zionism, feminism, civil rights, and we celebrated the Jewish holidays in a way that I could enjoy. And we cared for one another. Hillel was our madrich. I remember reading and discussing "The Feminine Mystique" with him and our kvutza. It opened my mind, but it took me years to integrate the message. After Hillel made aliyah, Natan Yonatan became our madrich and his love of Hebrew and Israel were a strong influence. My friends in the movement opened me up to art, alternative cinema, theater, and the city. Between activities on Friday nights and Sundays we hung out in the Village, and visited museums and Central Park. I would stay over on the weekends at sleepovers at Tamar, Mimi, Andi and Shuli's homes. I would come to the ken straight after school on Fridays and make the trip back Sunday nights on the last train – back to reality and Rockville Centre. Summers at Shomria were a wonderful experience and gave me the opportunity to meet HH members from the other kenim.

I went on the '64-'65 Seminar to Dalia. I had just turned 17. I couldn't wait to get to Israel. I was able to graduate a year early from high school by going to summer school in Monticello. I took the bus from Liberty with Shuli every day.

When I arrived in Israel I immediately felt that I was home. I felt a sense of freedom and lightness and belonging I had never felt in the States. I spent my free weekends visiting families and places around the country. I was devastated when we left in January. I spent the next year plotting for a way to get back to Israel in any way possible. I was still only 17 and my parents were strongly opposed.

I went to Queens College commuting from Long Island and dreaming of Israel. I applied to the Hebrew University in Jerusalem and was accepted to the Archaeology and the Jewish History Depts. I made aliyah on my own in August 1966, after spending the summer in Shomria. I had also gone to Perth to help set up their camp, to say goodbye to the Canadian friends I had made on Seminar.

I loved living in Jerusalem and the '67 and '73 wars only intensified those feelings and my feelings of belonging.

I spent the '67 war on Gal-On. As I had been sponsored by the movement when I made aliyah, I had a room on the kibbutz that I shared with Shuli, and spent most weekends there. When Ariel Horowitz organized a group of foreign students who were living in the dorms with me at the university, I joined them. We were taught to load and shoot old WWII Czech rifles to participate in the defense of the kibbutz! There was a feeling that the kibbutz might be attacked. All the men had been called up and we spent the war helping to pick apples. I saw the way the kibbutz members treated the volunteers and I knew enough Hebrew by then to understand their judgmental comments. Kibbutz felt like a provincial small town and I had fallen in love with living in the city and with Jerusalem. I left the kibbutz and hitchhiked back to the empty dorms in the closed university as soon as I could.

The years I spent in Jerusalem from 1966 to 1974 were magical. I remember walking from my apartment in Kiryat Moshe to the Old City and the Western Wall, on the first day it was opened to the public. Soldiers stood above us on the ramparts, guarding us from snipers. I remember watching the snow falling outside the Archaeology Dept. library windows in 1968 for the first time in 27 years. What an incredible sight! Only one foot of snow fell, but the city was totally unprepared and was cut off from the rest of the country. We wandered the

streets greeting one another with Happy Snow Day!   We roamed the alleys in the
Old City, went to parties in Ein Karem, went to crazy Purim parties at the Betzalel
Art Academy, had lunch in Ramallah by an indoor fountain with friends from East
Jerusalem, hung out in the bar in Beit HaOmanim after proofreading the next
day's edition of the Jerusalem Post. We sat in Ta'amon with friends from Matzpen
and went to Black Panther demonstrations.

Friends from the movement slowly made their way to Jerusalem.   It was always
fun to bump into them and catch up but I was busy becoming Israeli.

Those were difficult years, financially. My parents had cut me off and at times I
worked 3 part-time jobs to make ends meet. But I was happy and felt an intense,
visceral, and spiritual connection to Jerusalem. I became totally opposed to the
occupation almost immediately after my initial euphoria after the '67 war, and
became active politically.

In 1974 I married Uri and we left Israel for Los Angeles where we attended
graduate school. Our plan initially was to return to Israel after completing our
studies. It took 19 years, and 3 children but we returned in 1993 after Oslo. We
were filled with optimism!

I had yearned to return to Israel all the years we lived in LA. I never felt at home
there. I worked mainly in Jewish institutions as a way to feel closer to Israel. My
first job in LA was in the Hebrew Union College library, where I was able to use
my Hebrew and my degrees in archaeology and Jewish history. I went to night
school while working full-time in the library, and got a Master's Degree in Library
Science from USC. A few years later I began working at the Simon Wiesenthal
Center, at first in their library, and later I spent a few years doing research and
writing the content for an exhibition for their planned Museum of Tolerance.
Working in those places only reinforced my desire to return to Israel. I joined a
synagogue to give my children a sense of their Jewish heritage, but I have never
felt comfortable with organized religion. My children weren't really interested.
Understandably they wanted to be like everyone around them.

The first years in Israel were difficult. The boys, aged 7, 12 and 15 at the time,
didn't know Hebrew. We didn't have jobs. We lived off the money we had gotten
from selling our house in LA. Slowly but surely we both eventually found
fulfilling work and our children adjusted.

I haven't regretted for a moment returning to Israel. My three sons, who are now
in their mid-30s and early 40s live and work in Tel Aviv. The oldest went to the
army. The two youngest didn't. They all flirted with the idea of leaving. All three
spent time in the States and quickly returned to Israel. I see them and my

grandkids (I have five – and one more about to make an appearance) every week.

I am extremely distressed about the way this country has become more right-wing and under the influence of the ultra-orthodox. I will continue to express my feelings about this at the polls and at demonstrations. During this past Covid-19 year, I've only gone to very small demonstrations in Karkur – to stay socially-distanced and healthy.

Since my return to Israel, and the concurrent rise of the Internet, I've been able to reconnect and spend time with some of my friends from the movement. We still have lots to talk about, and feel a strong bond and a closeness that still amazes and fills me with joy.

Baruch Fischhoff

I grew up in a very stable, very Jewish neighborhood in Northwest Detroit. Vernor Elementary (named after the ginger ale magnate) might have been 90% Jewish, Mumford High, perhaps 60%. Our family time was spent in enclaves that arrived from Lithuania (mother's side) before World War I and Hungary just afterward. My father was born in Budapest.

We didn't belong to a congregation, for financial reasons, I assume. At the time, before the rise of congregational schools, the United Hebrew Schools served the non-Orthodox. It was a ¾ mile trudge from Vernor to 7 Mile and Schaeffer, four afternoons a week and twice the trudge from home (each way) on Sundays (and Shabbat for the final year). My mother's father probably facilitated a bar mitzvah, joint with my cousin Paul (who passed away recently) at his synagogue, Beth Aaron. On the high holidays, we would go with my father's father to a mysterious moving congregation, which met for a few years at the National Guard Armory on 8 Mile near Southfield. Tanks and half-tracks lined the entryway. We had the first seder with my father's side of the family and the second with my mother's, featuring my Aunt Thelma's green kugel.

There was great affinity for Israel and JNF (Jewish National Fund) boxes, but little politics or talk about the Holocaust, even though many survivors found their way to Detroit. *Exodus* (paperback or movie) probably came about the same time as I discovered my father's father's copy of the *Black Book of Polish Jewry*. My first political activity, though, was meetings of CORE, in the basement of the (now closed) Detroit Public Library at 7 and James Couzens (now the John C. Lodge Freeway). Eli Greenbaum, a friend whose parents had been in the movement in Poland, got me to come along to a meeting of the tiny local Ken Negba, on Wyoming close to Mumford. He dropped out, but I was hooked.

Our shaliach was Yis Stashevski, a former Detroiter who had gone to Sasa. Our rosh ken was Tzvi Snitz (Barkai). Guy Koretz joined not long afterward. Assaf and Miri Orr, shlichim from 1966-68 or so, became friends for life. The Kalom sisters were there off and on, in from South Haven. Ye'ala (Lahav). Aviva Weiss. Others. We had a moshava that summer near Mackinac, then went to Perth after that. Perth had a six-week session, so the older people drove to Liberty, which ran two weeks longer. I first met Andi there, when we were 15 and 16. Ken Negba had its own Mosh Choref, with the shlichim worrying about the bills. There were trips to the chava and the first seminar on Dalia, with Mordy Hahn as our chaperone (flight to Paris, train to Marseilles, SS Theodore Herzl to Haifa).

As with everyone who stayed in the movement for a while, there was something magical about being taken seriously by older people (madrichim and shlichim) and each other, as well as the sense of collective purpose. But the travel together was a big part of the adventure, especially for someone from the provinces, with no money to speak of and movement duties that precluded earning more as a wage slave. Who today lets their teens do things like hitchhiking to Quebec City with Natan Kalb, the last leg with the proud owner of Roberto's Boneless Chicken? It was a different time. And we were lucky that nothing went too badly wrong.

The President of Temple Beth Israel, in Eugene, once told me that he had taken on the job, despite being an atheist, as his contribution to preserving the liturgical music. I have never found the zone where some people get great value from the repetitiveness of prayers. However, I do love some of the melodies learned at United Hebrew School and a very few more recent ones.

At work, I think that Judaism, as filtered through the movement, has had a big imprint. Outside of work, my chronicle is not that different from Andi's for the last fifty-some years, just without her remarkable community contacts and organizing ability.

Bonnie (Plutzer) Ellinger - My Jewish Life

My Jewishness is intricately tied up with HH and Israeli-ness. My maternal and paternal grandparents' homes were English-speaking, although they knew Yiddish well and kept kosher. Both my grandmothers arrived in the US at the age of six months. My parents could "get along" in Yiddish, when they needed to, but our home was neither religious nor Jewish in any obvious way (no shul-going, for example) and not kosher. My older brother began studying Hebrew for his Bar Mitzvah but eventually gave up since he didn't care for the rabbi's punitive methods of getting the language across. My left-leaning folks were involved with other leftist friends, among whom were the parents of Ricky Friedman and Jimmy Larkin. When my parents were looking for a summer camp for my brother and me in 1959 (he was 15 and I was 11), they consulted with a friend named Dick Yaffe, who was the editor of "Israel Horizons", so off we went to Shomria. Moshava was a great fit for me but not for my brother. During the first week of camp (as my parents were enjoying a long-awaited vacation in Mexico), Marty broke his leg playing softball. The unfortunate accident signaled the end of an even minimally Jewish life for him since he spent the next six weeks in our sweltering two-family house in Brooklyn while his leg healed.

Of course, my involvement in the movement was just beginning, and in 1965, after graduating from high school, I went on Seminar to Kibbutz Galon and Kibbutz Mishmar HaEmek. While on Galon I met Avraham, whom I later married. After a few months on the kibbutz, we decided to move to NY, where my son Elan was born. It was a difficult time for various reasons, so we returned to the kibbutz where we stayed together for another couple of years until we divorced. In 1972 I left the kibbutz with Elan to a not-very-well-defined future. What I did know was that I had to get an education and bring up Elan as best I could. There was no discussion of returning to the States at that time.

What was my Jewish life like during my 35 years in Israel (1967-2002)?

In Israel you are Jewish by default. During my years on kibbutz (1967-72), we lived a secular Israeli and (more or less) socialist life with a dismissive attitude towards religion. This approach fit in well with the principles we had absorbed in HH in our formative adolescent years. Among the kibbutz members were the vatikim, some of whom had arrived in Israel in the 30s and established the kibbutz and others who had survived the Holocaust. When we were on Seminar, we were given adoptive families who were both welcoming and curious about these (spoiled?) American kids who were spending time in their communal home. My "original" kibbutz parents, survivors, were lovely people and we got along well, but when I lived on Galon as a married member, there was another couple that I wished would "adopt" me. After broaching the subject, I made the switch, and everyone seemed fine with it. I guess my better instincts were working, because I understood that I could, and did, have a very meaningful relationship with Bella and Chaim (who met on the Exodus). They were loving, wise survivors who treated Elan as their own grandchild, and I was a young mother *in need of* a mother. My own mother said many times that she was so glad that Bella had become my second mother. With Chaim I talked about classical music and from Bella I learned about her experiences during the war. She was an only child growing up in Lithuania and spent the years from age 16-20 in Bergen Belsen. She never saw her parents again after they were separated. On Yom HaShoah, on the kibbutz, the family would gather in their cheder and have a memorial service. I recall the first Yom HaShoah that I spent with them. There was a photo of Bella and her parents, one on each side of her, taken shortly before they were rounded up. Knowing Bella's story about her life in the camp, I was amazed to see that she had salvaged a photo. When I asked her how that could be, she told me it had been hidden in her shoe for the four years she had spent in the camp. Tragically, Bella died at age 48.

When I left the kibbutz, I found an apartment for my son and me across the street from Bar Ilan University (BIU). I had never heard of Bar Ilan, but it suited me to take courses and be a short distance from Elan's kindergarten and school while doing so. The studies that began at Bar Ilan in 1972 developed into a long-term relationship with the place where I ended up doing all my degrees and teaching for 20 years.

Bar Ilan was my first real contact with Orthodox Judaism outside of my grandparents' homes. Due to the nature of the university, I was required to take courses in Tanach, Talmud, and Jewish philosophy along with the literature and linguistic studies for my degrees. I found most of the Jewish Studies courses intriguing and I made many religious friends. I benefited from a Jewish education that I would not have gotten had I studied somewhere else. After completion of my B.A., I was fortunate to get an English teaching job at Thelma Yellin Music and Art HS in Givatayim. I taught there for eight years while concurrently doing my M.A. It was uplifting to begin my teaching career in such a creative, artistic environment, since I had had an upbringing filled with music and appreciated working with teenagers who were developing their expressive/imaginative sides along with their knowledge of English. After finishing my M.A. I returned to Bar Ilan to teach and pursue a Ph.D. Although the policy of BIU was generally to hire those who led a "religious" (i.e. a Shomer Shabbat) way of life, I was accepted for who I was and had very fruitful years there. I was somewhat uncomfortable living in a sea of religiosity (especially when political subjects came up), but the enjoyment of teaching and engaging with my students made up for any discomfort.

In 2002, while on sabbatical in Seville, Spain, I met Paul and made the decision to take early retirement and move to Santa Fe, NM where Paul was living. At the Spanish language school where we were studying, 90% of the students were 20–30-year-olds, usually very tall, Europeans, but here we were, two former east coast Jews, close in age, both living in the old Jewish ghetto of Seville, intent on enhancing our Spanish – and getting to know one another.

After 35 years in Israel, returning to the US was a pretty dramatic change, but it was made easier by the fact that at that very same time Elan and his young family were relocating for three years to Istanbul and then to Seattle for his work at Microsoft which had begun in Israel.

I needed to maintain my Jewish/Israeli identity in Santa Fe, but how?

Shortly after my arrival in New Mexico, I began teaching English at one of the local colleges. It was a completely different experience from my professional life in Israel and much less satisfying. As I got to know more people in town, I was asked if I could teach Hebrew. That query led to 14 years of my new career of holding Hebrew classes for various groups of adults. Very few people were interested in conversational Hebrew. There was no great rush to make aliyah among the Jews of Santa Fe. The most common request was from those who wanted to follow the religious services at the local congregations. I even taught at Chabad for a year which prompted an Orthodox friend of mine in Israel to comment: if Bonnie is teaching for Chabad, the Messiah must have come! I loved my new profession. It filled me with joy to be able to preserve my connection to Hebrew and Israel by helping others to see the logic and beauty of the language. I felt privileged to be able to do so.

In addition to those years of teaching, I became very involved in the newly established Santa Fe Jewish Film Festival as well as the also new Santa Fe Distinguished Lecture Series. By teaching Hebrew and being part of these two groups, I have been able to live a culturally stimulating Jewish life in a place where I can comfortably express myself on issues related to my Jewishness and Israel. Since Santa Fe is a relatively small city, I feel that my Jewish voice counts.

Santa Fe, NM
February 2021

Claudia Tublin aka Chedva

It's great to reconnect after so many years. Ira, thanks for communicating with me about the zoom meeting. Uri, I enjoyed your amusing stories. Dorothea, your writings brought back memories of my childhood and my father's journey, although not the same experiences. I have never been comfortable writing but will try to give some idea of how I came to Hashomer Hatzair.

I grew up in Crown Heights, Brooklyn NY in an apartment building. My father came from Poland (Volynia now in Ukraine) in 1929 at the age of 19. My mother was born in Brooklyn. We were not religious but celebrated the holidays and Shabbat.

I have vivid memories of a child's book of Bible stories illustrated by Gustave Dore that my father gave me.

All my childhood friends were Jewish. My next door neighbor led the children's service at a synagogue on Eastern Parkway and I went with my friends. I never felt religious but felt strongly Jewish. My family was progressive and I had a liberal upbringing. There were art books and fine literature in the house, classical and folk music. My mother took my sister and me to museums, the ballet, and opera.

When I started junior high I became interested in civil rights and ban the bomb. I used to go to Washington Square and join the folk singing. I even met Bob Dylan before he was famous. I came to Hashomer by chance. A friend invited me. She didn't continue but I did. It felt good to be part of a group that shared some of the values I had and I felt a strong connection that being Jewish has a historic connection to Israel. I loved learning Hebrew songs and dances. The idealism of kibbutz was attractive. To leave the city and be in nature, I loved Camp Shomria. After I joined I found out that my father was a member of Hashomer Hatzair in Poland. He almost went to Palestine but his whole family had emigrated to the United States before him, so he ended up in Brooklyn. One of my father's brothers went to Israel in the 1950s and found relatives who settled in Palestine in 1902. This increased my interest and desire to go to Israel.

Although I did not stay in Israel I still feel a connection and believe strongly in its existence. I married a man of Italian background but my son is named Meir after my father and we celebrate Jewish holidays and I have shared my Jewish experience and culture. My grandchildren are a mix of Jewish, Italian and El Salvadorian, and I share the Jewish holiday's food. They love latkes and matzah balls. I sing the the few songs I remember from Hashomer, especially Natan Yonatan's that Tzfira taught us.

So nice to hear your voices again,

Chedva

David Mencher – Jerusalem - Brooklyn, NY
WHERE AM I AND HOW DID I GET HERE?

In HH, we were taught to believe that Israel, and particularly kibbutz, was the answer. Sixty years later, I now know that asking the question is often the most important thing. And HH did not make clear what the question was/is or should be.

I grew up in Brooklyn, in an English and Yiddish speaking household, which included my grandparents (Workmen Circle members from Bialystok in Poland), my American-born, socialist/communist parents, an older sister and a younger brother. Although exclusively Jewish holidays were celebrated, and wonderful European Jewish food predominated, religion played no part in our upbringing. Brit mila, bar mitzvahs yes, attempts at fasting on Yom Kippur, but shul or mitzvoth were absent. I was brought up as, and remain to this day, an atheist.

In HH I thought I had found a way to give expression to my sense of Jewishness, without having to question my atheism. As we were preparing to live the life of the "new Jewish pioneer" on kibbutz, it was even okay to poke fun at religion, and point out the many contradictions in the bible. We were so smart.

Fast forward to early 1980s – I am living in Jerusalem, married to Dvora, a bat kibbutz from Gal On, whose mother Madga z"l has passed away from cancer. Funeral on the kibbutz, I look around and I am left feeling empty, with no sense of tradition within which to contain the personal as well as collective mourning. I begin to understand then, the importance for me of tradition and ritual for the marking of significant events in the cycle of life. Important, even for an atheist.

Fast forward to Portland, OR, 1990-95. I am a chiropractic student and an "adopted" member of the Feuer family (Dina and Yaaki z"l and their kids and grandchildren), immensely enjoying their loose, Carlebach-style Shabbat dinners, Jewish holidays and Israel/Jewish-centered lifestyle. Knowing Hebrew already, the prayers and bible passages I encounter in the Kabbalat Shabbat and occasional visits to bet knesset are now partially decipherable, and pique my curiosity.

Back in Israel, starting 1995 – now I miss the traditions of the Portland years, and am lucky enough to be introduced to a special kehila in Baka, Jerusalem, Kol HaNeshama, and Rabbi Levy Wyman-Kelman. Levy understood what the authors of The Jew and the Lotus concluded from their journey to discover the source of Buddhism's attraction for Jewish baby boomers – that post-enlightenment orthodoxy had usurped "Jewish spiritualism" and that Jews outside of the pale of orthodoxy needed to regain a connection with spiritual, emotional and collective aspects of Jewish tradition. Levy, and his congregation at Kol HaNeshama, provided me and my kids with another opportunity to encounter Jewish tradition and culture, without abandoning my atheism.

Fast forward 25 years – still an atheist, and now much more confident of my place in the spectrum of Jewish tradition. Living here in Israel, I feel free to join in traditions when and how I please, to learn about our history, and live with a sense of being part of the continuum of Jewish existence, and part of this historic experiment which is Israel. Judy, my partner (one of the founding members of Kehilat Kol HaNeshama), keeps kosher, and I can be comfortable with keeping a kosher home in deference to her preferences and in order to be able to host religious friends. I find interest in discussing bible passages with knowledgeable friends, especially around Pesach and other holidays, and am always ready to learn and understand more. But without any pressure to believe, or conform to anyone else's idea of what Jewish life should be like. I feel very fortunate.

And so, I return to the "question" – for me the "question", which I believe takes a lifetime to ask is, "Where do I belong in this continuum of history and tradition that I am and want to be a part of?"

Make no mistake – this is not a uniquely Jewish question. Many aspects of one's identity (religious, cultural, gender, political, social, professional and more) offer endless opportunities for reflection and re-evaluation. Looking for the answers has brought me great satisfaction.

David Mencher

Jerusalem
February 7, 2021

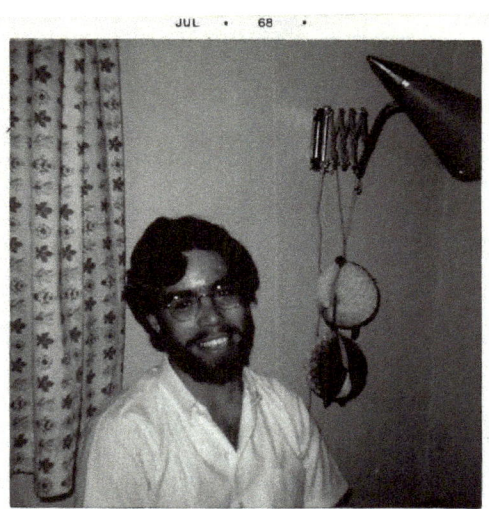

Yehuda, Lilit, David, Dvora, Yechiel in Jerusalem

Donnie Goldstein – Career Advisor at the CUNY Graduate Center
Brooklyn, New York

In 1963, I was a sophomore at James Madison High School in Brooklyn. I was an average student who was totally unmotivated and disinterested. I really disliked school. I had a nice group of neighborhood friends — all boys, kids I had grown up with. We played a lot of ball in the street and in the schoolyard. We went bowling, we went out for pizza, and we played nickel and dime poker games. I read a lot and I spent a good deal of time in the library. I worked part-time as a stock boy at the Howard Clothes store in downtown Brooklyn. My mother was a stay-at-home mom taking care of me and my brother and my father worked as an official for the Amalgamated Clothing Workers Union. Politically, my whole family was staunch liberal Democrats. We were secular Jewish. I had gone to Hebrew School at a Reform Temple, had a Bar Mitzva and never went back again. We observed some of the major Jewish holidays with my nearby extended family as festive non-religious occasions. We never read the Hagada, we just ate. We were proud of Israel but it rarely came up in family conversations and the idea of going there to live was about as likely as going to the Moon.

It's amazing how one totally mundane day can change your life forever. That's the day I met a skinny red-headed kid named Joey Appel in high school. We started to hang out together and he told me about a "club" that he belonged to. He said that it was like the Jewish Boy Scouts except that they had discussions about current events and Israel and that it was coed and the girls were very pretty. He said I should come and it would be fun. It all sounded good to me especially that part about pretty girls.

It took a few meetings and I was hooked on the friendships, the identification with the heroic and beleaguered Israel, the equality and social justice of the kibbutz movement, and the left-wing politics.

Also, did I mention that there were pretty girls? — but girls who were smart, friendly, and approachable and that helped me to get out from under my extreme shyness.

In 1965, I attended the seminar on Gal On and Mishmar HaEmek. It was so exciting. I had never been further than Washington D.C. and I had never been on an airplane before. We met a group of American Shomrim who had come to Israel in the 1950s and built their lives together on the kibbutz — real life role models. I learned a little Hebrew and learned how to work — hard, physical outdoor work in the blistering August heat, and we took amazing trips. I'm glad I got to see the poor, endangered, idealistic pre-1967 Israel.

When I got back from seminar I became more involved in Hashomer Hatzair. Between 1966-69, I was a Madrich, Mazkir Galil New York, Rosh Machene at Moshava, Rosh Ken in the Bronx and Mazkir T'nua. I learned skills at a pretty early age that served me very well throughout the rest of my life. The most important was communication in many forms. I wrote letters, articles, press releases and fliers and learned to write in a clear, concise way. Later on in my career, I would be writing emails, reports, case notes and studies, articles, blog pieces, programming proposals, and publicity descriptions for workshops. Another form of communication is public speaking. I, being an extreme introvert, was terrified of standing up and speaking in front of a group of people. As Mazkir T'nua, I had to do that dozens of times so I was already honing skills that I would use later on in delivering workshops and teaching classes. Speaking of education, I adopted the experiential hands-on and collaborative Hashomer Hatzair education philosophy. I learned that kids needed to be interested and engaged in order to learn. I always look at a class or a workshop as a peulah rather than a lecture and employ a number of different methodologies including discussions, group work, role-playing, debates, and imaginative play.

I also did a lot of event planning in Hashomer. My first activity as Mazkir Galil was an ice-skating activity in Central Park. It was early March and I just assumed that the Wollman Rink was open until April 1. It wasn't. Luckily the other Madrichim turned it into a field day. The day was saved but it was so embarrassing and humiliating that I vowed that my lack of attention to detail would never happen again and it never did.

The Chava was a difficult episode for me. The equipment was old, run down and falling apart. Kibbutz Lahav did not have any of the branches that we had on the Chava and there were social fissures within our group. During the summer of 1969, men walked on the Moon, the miracle Mets won the World Series, and thousands of youth converged on Woodstock, but we could not get the silage into the silo.

There were a number of heart-wrenching sichot and a lot of hurt feelings and the Chava closed in December, 1969. I knew that it was inevitable, but I carried that guilt of failure with me for a long time.

The tragedy of that summer though was the death of Yehuda Krantz. Yehuda was an enormously bright and dynamic 17-year-old who often stayed over at the apartment that I shared with Steve Weinstein and Joey Beinin in Washington Heights.

Because of the closing of the Chava, we dribbled into Kibbuz Lahav in ones, twos, and threes. By this point, I had realized that there were other viable alternatives in life besides going to Israel and living on a kibbutz, but I had invested so much in it already, that I felt that I had to see it through. The Kibbutz wasn't ready for us and we weren't ready for them. There were problems around hashish smoking and army service. We lived on the outskirts of the Kibbutz and many members couldn't distinguish us from the volunteers. Some of the members were downright prejudiced and unfriendly towards Americans. In my naivete, I remember feeling disappointed that many of the members were just regular folk dealing with mundane life issues and not the high caliber intellectual and ideological shlichim. It all seemed so small town.

I got married to a sabra and lived on Lahav for three years. I worked in falcha and I was in the best shape of my life. I got to experience the longest lasting and most successful communal experiment of the 20th Century. I met many warm and wonderful people including kibbutz members, volunteers and two amazing Bedouin that I worked with in falcha.

I did wind up living another eight years in Israel in Jerusalem where I was a community worker and a social science researcher for the Joint Distribution Committee and the Municipality of Jerusalem. After my divorce, I returned to Brooklyn where I still live. I have a son and two grandchildren in Petach Tikva and I used to visit Israel quite often before the Pandemic.

In the mid 90s, for four years, I served as the editor of Israel Horizons, the venerable API, Mapam, and then Meretz quarterly magazine. I have stayed close to Hashomer Hatzair through Linda Rubin, who is the COO of the Givat Haviva Foundation. She also handles the finances for Camp Shomria and for a number of years, we have gone up there on just a regular day without it being a reunion or a Parent's Day. It has been heartwarming to see the present day Shomrim enjoying the same type of friendships and learning the values and life skills that we took away from the Movement. My daughter, Alyssa attended Camp Shomria for six summers and thankfully Survival Day was no longer a thing.

I think one should also learn from mistakes. We were often too heavy-handedly involved in people's lives and were too smug and judgmental. I regret that we expelled one of my best friends from Hashomer when a better solution could have been found. I am embarrassed by the sexism that we boys displayed. When the boys rented a Carry All and took a trip to Eilat during the seminar, it was never even a consideration that the girls should come too. On the Chava, while women worked in the lul and refet, only women had the tasks of shopping, cooking, and cleaning the bayit. There were certainly many other ways that sexism was conveyed and I do feel ashamed about that. On the other hand, I do think that we believed and acted upon values and ideals that were worthy — cooperation, communal values like kupah, the dignity of physical labor, taking responsibility, and progressive political ideals and values.

The greatest treasure that I took away from Hashomer Hatzair are the life-long friendships that started at Ken Masada, Moshava, the Chava and the Kibbutz. Almost all of my best friends are the people I came of age with during those shared experiences and that group has expanded to include spouses, partners, and children — friends that are like family.

It is now more than 57 years since I first set foot in Ken Masada. Whatever fate that landed me in the same class with Joey Appel — I thank my lucky stars.

Donnie emerging from a bunker on Kibbutz Dan — Seminar 1965

Donnie with Elana Tucker and Linda Rubin at a reunion at Camp Shomria in Liberty, NY

Dorothea Dorenz – My Connection to My Jewish Identity and Beginnings in HH 2/11/21

My grandfather was a Rebbe, a teacher who ran a school that prepared yeshiva bochers for their Bar Mitzvahs in Bialostok, Poland. My father, a budding artist, would sit in his father's "cheder" and doodle in the margins of his chumash (Torah in book form), while his older brothers plotted to overthrow the Czar. At the age of ten he was hiding guns in the rafters of the family home. With the failure of the 1905 revolution, the family planned to immigrate.

My father's older brother was supposed to check out Palestine as a possible immigration destination, and give a report to my grandfather, but when he got to Odessa to board a boat headed for Palestine, an old, long-bearded, Yid came up to him asking if he wanted to go to Eretz Yisrael, and that he would help him buy his ticket for the boat. Sadly, my Uncle Charlie gave him the money, and this helpful Yid disappeared. So Charlie never got to check out Palestine, and the family, one by one, all ten of them, immigrated to the U.S. along with 3 million other Jews as a result of the Kishniev pogroms, and the then open-door U.S. immigration policy.

My father David, an artist and a Communist, threw out religious Judaism, but he identified strongly as Jewish. He read the Forward in Yiddish, along with Yiddish poetry and had me attend a Jewish School to learn Yiddish. My sister and I never did learn much Yiddish. He never taught me Torah, or anything about religious thought. I don't think he realized that his new "religion", communism, had its underpinnings in Torah, and Jewish ethics. The *one* time my father decided to bring my sister and I to a synagogue was on Rosh Hashana. We marched up to a shul in Jackson Heights only to be told at the door that we needed to buy a ticket. My infuriated father told us that religion should not be for sale, so we turned around and went straight back home!

My mother was a first generation Jew who knew very little about Judaism and didn't show any curiosity about it until much later in her life when she started to learn Hebrew and attended the Jewish community center in Queens. My father and my mother visited Israel after the Yom Kippur War. That war finally convinced my father that Russia was not to be trusted, and that was as close to becoming a Zionist as he ever came.

Growing up in an Irish Catholic neighborhood in Queens, I was always very aware that we were a "different" family: Jewish and Communist! These two identities had to be kept quiet, especially during the McCarthy years when the FBI came knocking at our door. Fortunately, my mom knew her rights and refused to answer their questions.

In Hashomer Hatzair, we also did not learn that Jewish learning was an inspiration for socialism, and I felt that something was missing when we celebrated the Jewish holidays as primarily agricultural holidays. That "something " wasn't god. I was an atheist and remain one, but now that I have studied some Torah and Mishnah, I know what was "missing": the knowledge of the sources of major Jewish ideas and ethics, and how the sources keep getting reinterpreted to deal with our current realities. I think that if we had learned our traditional sources in some way, it would have strengthened our attachment to Judaism, living a Jewish life, and Zionism, rather than the other way around. The secular New York Zionists of Hashomer Hatzair were afraid of creating that connection or ignorant of it. Still, being a shomeret, was a powerful emotional and educational experience! Being a madricha was a wonderful experience and gave me skills that I have used in my teaching of art, and my Self Healing Classes. It also taught me the importance of community. On Seminar in Mishmar HaEmek I read a lot about the Holocaust which had an enormous effect on my world view, sensitivity to antisemitism, and understanding of the need for a Jewish State.

Growing up in an Irish Catholic neighborhood in Queens meant I was perhaps one of four Jews in my elementary school: Eydie (Tamar), Michael Fishman, and Jeffery Cerini, were the other three. Michael invited us to a Friday night gathering at the Ken and I was hooked. I was so glad to have a social group to relate to with songs, dancing, and hilarity. Being Jewish has been very important to me throughout my life. My Jewish background has made finding work easier, first through help by my Jewish mother-in-law, then, after I got my graduate degree in art, I was able to get a job as soon as I landed in San Francisco as art director of the San Francisco Jewish Home, a large retirement home now called The San Francisco Campus for Jewish Living.

After quitting HH to join the civil rights and anti war efforts, I rejoined at Natan Yonathan's urging so that I could go on Seminar in 1965 and see what Israel was like. On my return, I was appointed Rosh Ken, N'tiv Mordecai, in Queens. I was on the Hachshara where I was in charge of the refet, learned to milk cows and make sure they had lots of calves!! That "training" turned out to be out of date in regard to kibbutz life for women, but it taught me responsibility, and I loved the cows who all had names of different kinds of whiskey given to them by previous shomrim!!!

I made Aliyah in 1968 to Gal On, but returned to New York to attend my sister Nina's wedding. When I left to make aliyah I knew that she had leukemia, and so when I returned for the wedding, it was hard to go back to Israel. I hadn't established my roots there yet, and I was not attracted to agricultural work even though I spent almost a year on the chava getting ready for kibbutz life. It's hard to get the city out of a New Yorker, and to see how, on kibbutz, women were demoted to the same housekeeping type jobs that we were trying to free ourselves from in the U.S. Still, it was a very good experience, and I loved learning Hebrew, which I continue to study today. My plan before my sister's wedding was to leave the kibbutz to attend art school in Israel. Instead, I returned to Queens College to get my degree in painting and drawing.

Judaism took a back seat for a long time in my middle years. During graduate school in Baton Rouge, it never even occurred to me to attend a synagogue. But later in Berkeley, as a mom, I wanted my son to have a sense of belonging around his Jewish identity and Judaism, similar to what I had in HH: to be a member of a Jewish group, and to be proud of his identity. Although I never became Bat Mitzvah, I wanted him to learn about Judaism and have a Bar Mitzvah. If one belongs to a synagogue in the U.S., it helps one to be part of a Jewish community, so I joined a Jewish Renewal synagogue that was eventually led by Rabbi David Cooper who had been a chaniach of Teddy Vermont's in HH!

The Renewal version of Judaism is very different from traditional Judaism. This shul was very welcoming to LGBTQ people, it changed the gender specifications for the prayers, and also reinvented the prayers. But I became curious about what traditional Judaism was like. What kept our people going for so many centuries? So I joined a Conservative shul in Berkeley and found my niche as chair of the Israel Committee. This tied up some important threads in my life: Israel, Judaism, leadership, and education.

Before my marriage I explored Buddhism and after my marriage I explored Hindu meditation. Both of these practices gave me insight into different ways to live. Unlike the Judaism that I knew, they teach the practical tools of meditation as a means of knowing oneself and others. Current day Judaism in the US now teaches meditation that is closer to the idea of Buddhist meditation. Hinduism offered a kind of comfort that Judaism, for me, still lacks. I can't relate to the constant "praise god" aspects of the Jewish prayer services, but I can relate to the human aspiration to live up to the values of living as compassionate human beings who cherish the lives of others, and work to make the world a more just place. I now understand that we Jews need the particularist attachment to our Jewish identities along with our universalist values. But the world is not ready for universalism which means we have to know who we are. Judaism keeps me thinking, but it is not a "comforting" religious practice for me. It's more of an intellectual endeavor.

I have never been a god believer, and don't need a god belief to be Jewish. Judaism is a religion/philosophy and an ethnicity. I have done and still study some Torah to discover more about our religion that has hugely influenced the two largest religions in the world, Christianity and Islam. Judaism also has influenced Western secular thought regarding justice, time, caring for others, and so much more. I want to understand why this religion has had so much influence on others. I enjoy reading Rabbi Sacks' z"l drashot which are always relevant to what we are living through today.

I can be Jewish and choose what I want to observe ritually, but for me the most important thing is continuing to learn about this complex religion, our history, and how Zionism has evolved into being one of the newest forms of Judaism that continues to evolve both in Israel and in the United States.

What preoccupies me now: I am very concerned that our young people in the U.S. are assimilating at a high rate including my own son. Having a clear identity makes one strong as does belonging to a group whose values match your own in some ways. Many Jews in the U.S. don't have a clue as to what Judaism is about. With the growth of Jew hate in this country they may face a rude awakening, as did the Jews in Germany. I see it happening already.

The split here over Israel is very painful for me to see, and it goes so far as to have Jews on the left completely abandoning any connection to Israel. Some of their disaffection is based on disappointed idealism: Israel was supposed to be better than other nation states, and somehow magically survive in a very hostile environment without playing by the rules of self-defense in order to do so. Although I was raised to be an idealist, I am a realist. I have met some disappointed idealists who have become some of the most anti-Zionist people that I have met. Perhaps they don't know the history of our ancestors' centuries of oppression that culminated in the Holocaust, or they think they are perpetually safe here in the United States, which negates in their minds the need for Israel after the Holocaust and today as the home of 45% of world Jewry.

In the last few years, I have worked with others to fight Jew hate that is definitely on the rise in the U.S. I am a member of Zioness, which was formed when many Jewish women discovered that we are unwelcome in the Women's Movement and other progressive causes, because we are accused of being white supremacists. If you love Israel, you are not welcome in any so-called "progressive" movement.

Organizations on the left recently came out against the International Holocaust Memorial Alliance's definition of antisemitism becoming a legal document, which it is not and never will be. I see this stance that they are taking as a "red herring". The IHRA definition does not stifle free speech as these groups claim. The fact that there is now a definition of antisemitism is something that we Jews should be *very happy* about, and that 31 countries have signed onto it including the U.S. that did so in 2010. Those organizations opposing it include J Street, an organization of liberal Rabbis, and sadly, Hashomer Hatzair. Biden just came out in full support of this definition that doesn't stifle free speech, as those that oppose it claim, but educates Jews and non-Jews with a clear definition of antisemitism in all of its iterations. If people don't know what it is, then they can't stand up against it. This is the first time in history that world governments have decided that it's time to commit to fighting antisemitism. I am working to form a group of people in my synagogue who are interested in fighting Jew hate in whatever ways we can, and have worked to counter the antisemitism that has cropped up on the right, the left and in between.

I hope that the divisions in the Jewish community and assimilation will not result in a desertion of Israel and a further disavowal of Judaism, which I see as very dangerous for both. Israel as a nation and as a homeland for Jews, needs, and is influenced by the U.S. and it seems that the U.S. needs Israel as an ally in the

Middle East, and for sure, U.S. Jews need Israel! The various streams of Judaism in the U.S. are starting to have an affect on some secular Israelis who are now learning their Jewish heritage without becoming Charedim! With the disappearance of socialist kibbutzim, and the loss of socialist ethics, there is little to mitigate the soulless ultra capitalism in Israel that mirrors the heartless capitalism here in the U.S. Where will the ethics come from for both of our homelands??? One way I can see reversing this negative trend is to educate people in Jewish ethics.

My father, on his deathbed, told me, "I spent my whole life trying to understand man's inhumanity to man. If it weren't for antisemitism, Judaism would have disappeared a long time ago." He probably was right in part about the latter, but he didn't understand the role of Israel in the continued success and evolution of our Jewish identity, of Judaism, and of our people. If he were alive today, I think he would be astonished to see how Jews and Judaism continue to flourish here and in Israel. At the same time, he would be aghast at the re-emergence of virulent antisemitism in the United States and in Europe.

To my wonderful friends from HH: May all your paths be paths of peace!!
Dottee/Dorit/Dorothea

Dorothea, Andi and Marty Braff

Dov Gottdiener

I was born and grew up in the Bronx which has made me a life-long Yankees fan. My father and mother both managed to escape Europe in the late 30s and everyone from their families who remained in Europe perished in the Holocaust. My father was very religious and a scholar forced to be a laborer and my mother was a member of Beitar so it was inevitable that I joined HH.

Someone wrote that HH values were Zionism, Secular Judaism and Humanistic Socialism. Well, my calendar is the Jewish calendar. My work week is Sunday to Thursday, the holidays are the Jewish and Israeli holidays (Holocaust Day, Independence Day, Memorial Day, etc.) my language is Hebrew, the new movies and books I see and read are in Hebrew, besides English, so my identity is Israeli. My children grew up on kibbutz and were all in HH. My eldest son took a year off between high school and the army to work in HH and was Rosh Ken Kfar Sava. My grandchildren who are old enough are in Ken Galon and participate in all HH activities. All holidays are celebrated in a secular manner and the cultural life on Galon is very extensive. Anyone who can access Facebook in Hebrew can see videos of all the holidays and cultural events of the Kibbutz on קהילת גלאון. We all remain politically active, participating in the weekly Saturday night demonstrations against the current government. My two sons live on the Kibbutz and my daughter lives in Tel Aviv. Two work in HiTec and my oldest is a teacher and volunteer first responder. We all get together with the grandkids Friday night.

Significant changes have occurred in the ideology and structure of the kibbutz. Most have been the result of a society adjusting to the changing times both economically and socially (not within the scope of this short piece). But kibbutz is still a socialist economy, the means of production are owned equally by all members and the welfare and well-being of all is the top priority. However, there is a privatization of individual life. We own our houses and all new members build their own house. Members keep their income and pay municipal taxes and into funds to maintain equality. All members have a guaranteed income and pension and everyone is cared for in their old age.

These changes are part of a process that started more than 25 years ago and members of the garin were very instrumental in these changes which transformed Galon into a flourishing, dynamic and growing community that has an ever-growing waiting list of families that want to join us to have an Israeli, secular humanistic community. Galon has invested in alternative energy and has over 100 acres of solar power, a large part of the agriculture is organic. We live in a region that has been declared a green zone.
Best wishes to all.

Dov, Tzvi and Yehuda

Dvora Treisman (Bush/Buszejkin), Figueres, Catalonia, Spain

My parents were both from Warsaw. They were there when the Germans invaded in 1939 and my father, apparently trusting the Germans less than the Russians, headed towards where the Russians could be found. The rest of their families – all four of my grandparents, my mother's brother and two sisters – stayed and were exterminated.

My father was a handsome, blue-eyed blond and my mother a dark-haired, dark-eyed beauty. On their way fleeing the Germans, they were indeed stopped by a German patrol. One of the soldiers asked my father, "Isn't she Jewish?" and he replied, "Do you think I would carry on with a Jew?" My father wasn't an intellectual, but he knew up from down.

My mother's father was a Polish patriot, probably the only Jewish Polish patriot in Poland. He was a furrier. The family spoke Polish at home; they were middle class. I don't think they celebrated any of the Jewish holidays because my mother never seemed very familiar with Jewish customs. The one and only time she attempted to have a seder at our house, she served shrimp on the salad, to the horror of our assembled guests.

My father's father was a businessman. I believe he owned a tram line but he went bust sometime around 1932, recalled my father who was studying at the university in Montpellier at the time. The family was well-off bourgeois. I believe they also spoke Polish at home, although my father did know a little bit of Yiddish whereas I don't think my mother knew any and probably wouldn't have let on if she did.

His parents had sent my father to study medicine, but one look at a frog being dissected and he fainted. When he came back to, he promptly changed his field to agronomy. My dad was very athletic. In Poland he competed in boxing as a featherweight, skated, rode horses, and built up his muscles. He had a good time in Montpellier where he first started to smoke and went on long distance bike races, riding once to Barcelona.

In my home, stories about Russia had nothing to do with Marx or Lenin or communism. They had to do with the KGB and the Russian people. My father hated the KGB and loved the Russian people just as much as he disliked the Poles. In the end, they were grateful to the Russians. If not for them, they would have been exterminated together with the rest of their families. Instead, they spent the war working on a kolhoz in Siberia. Not much in the way of fun and games, but my father had studied agronomy and was put in charge of the farming, given a horse, and was in his element.

After the war, when they were repatriated, they found no family and Warsaw in ruins. So they decided to leave and went to Nice where my father had some kind of relative who owned a marmalade factory. They spent six months there working and waiting for their visas to go to the U.S.

When they landed in New York they found that they would not be allowed to stay. There was a quota for how many Jews could enter and they would have to wait their turn. So they went to wait in the Dominican Republic where Trujillo had made land and resources available for a colony of Jewish refugees, most of them Austrian. Not many people know about this colony in Sosua. It was agricultural, they had a dairy and they made cheese. My father was happy because he could once again use his agronomy skills. I have a photo of him sitting on his horse, surrounded by the corn he's grown that towers over his head. I also have several photos of me there as a baby, because this is where I was born. When, after two years, someone noticed that my father was an agronomist, they were put at the front of the line and soon got permission to enter the U.S. as residents.

We never celebrated Jewish holidays in my home. We celebrated Christmas and for Easter my mother would help me dye eggs which they would hide in the garden for me and my friends to find. But I knew we were Jewish. I knew I was Jewish. I knew it because all my family except my parents were killed just because they were Jewish. I knew it because I felt I owed it to them.

Hashomer presented me with a new perspective on being Jewish. I didn't join it for any ideological reason. I came with no particular interest in Judaism or socialism. My parents didn't send me. I joined because I had a crush on Jerry (Yoel) Krakowski, a family friend who was six years my senior and who had started attending meetings at Ken Nirim on Melrose Avenue in Los Angeles. My parents had met Jerry's parents when they were living in Russia during the war and the families had either stayed in touch or found one another again in the U.S. How people managed to do things like that when they were displaced and had no Internet I have no idea.

For me, Hashomer was a place to learn to sing and dance, make friends with people who shared my values and some of my history, gain self-confidence and come out of my shell, because I was a very shy girl. It was my village and I became a responsible member of it.

I didn't go on seminar to Kibbutz Dalya with my group because I graduated high school a year after the others – Shellie, Evie, Avi, and the rest. Later I met Uri at Shomria in Liberty. We went to the chava together but did not go on aliyah. Instead we went to live in Los Angeles so that Uri could finish the education he was so well suited to, planning to go to Israel when he had finished. We eventually moved to Berkeley for Uri to do graduate work and in the end we divorced and never did go on aliyah.

Many years later I married a Catalan and when he retired we came to live in Barcelona, his home town. Eventually we also divorced. I moved up to Figueres, Salvador Dali's home town near the French border and here I remain. I like it here, but I find it very difficult to be Jewish in a place where there are no other Jews. I'm not looking for a synagogue (there are four congregations in Barcelona, although that's two hours away). I want a deli; I want challah, seven-layer cake, and a knish; I want Chanuka candles; I want someone to kibbitz with someone who will understand what I'm saying without my having to go into hundreds of details of background to explain. Some years back, when I complained of this problem to Ami Isseroff, he said what did I expect? Spain threw the Jews out in 1492. Why did I feel compelled to be the first to come back?

So that's my history. Outside of Hashomer, I felt alienated in the U.S. I didn't feel American (the one time I felt very American was on September 11, after I had left, when I watched the airplane hit the twin towers on my television in Barcelona). Then I came to Catalonia and although I speak Catalan, am familiar with a lot of the history and culture, have learned some of the old songs, can dance the sardana, and have participated in the Catalan independence movement, I manage to feel alienated here. I have some new friends but no one close. I have my old friends. They all live in the U.S., but unlike my parents in their day, I have Internet and that makes it easier to stay in touch.

Baby Dvora and her parents

Eydie (Tamar) Kaufman Levy - Exploring my Heritage, or, The Jew Witch Question

For as long as I can remember, I have known that I am a Jew. I learned it in a cultural rather than a religious context. My family belonged to a people singled out by history and custom. We had our own calendar, foods, languages and humor. Sometimes, when I was very young, my grandmother would disappear into the bedroom of one of the Brooklyn apartments where we gathered for holidays, followed by my aunts and eldest female cousins. Later, I realized that the women were comforting my grandmother after she received official confirmation of the murder of yet another of her relatives in Europe. The shadow of the Shoah darkened those early years, though I became wary rather than fearful.

My father was an atheist, though his pride in Jews and Judaism bordered on chauvinism. He considered all organized religion oppressive, and all clergy to be parasites. He did not exclude rabbis from that judgment. Consequently, my parents never joined a synagogue. We had a Seder and Rosh HaShanah dinner with our extended family every year. The Passover story appealed to me, as did other biblical tales. My mother fasted on Yom Kippur but was vague when I asked her about her reasons. I went to services only when one of my older, male cousins would become a Bar Mitzvah. It was always an ordeal. I was unimpressed by the droning liturgy, and rolled my eyes when I heard the fulsome, rote praise that the professional rabbis lavished on the nervous boys.

I was a solitary, disaffected girl who lived in her imagination. It was Dorothea (Dottee/Dorit) who brought me to Hashomer Hatzair. There I found others similarly uneasy with the prevalent norms. They were intelligent, talented, idealistic, and tolerant of my idiosyncrasies. We sang, danced, schemed and dreamed together, and formed friendships that remain unequalled. My *madrichim*, beginning with Tzippy, educated me about Israel and Zionism. The romance of creating a utopian collectivist society in our ancient land was seductive. I left Hashomer Hatzair too soon, alas, and to this day regret not having gone on seminar when I had the chance.

My immersion in what has come to be called the counterculture of the 1960s led me to the study of yoga, astrology and Tarot. I had always been inclined towards myths and magic. I yearned for transcendence, and attempted to achieve it by various means. In my quest, I learned that there was a Jewish mystical tradition, replete with cosmic drama. My introduction to Kabbalah came through non-Jewish occultists, Theosophists and others. Its texts and practices were secret, guarded by Hasidim who believed that such teachings were dangerous. Only a pious, married man over forty, well-versed in Torah and Talmud, might delve into Kabbalistic realms without becoming unhinged. It was no wonder that secular, North American Jews had not heard of it. Nor was it part of the curriculum in the seminaries that provided vocational training for suburban pulpit rabbis.

The Jewish Renewal Movement increased my access to Kabbalah. I did not have to chant with the Buddhists, follow a Hindu guru, or whirl with the Sufis in order to experience spirituality. As Kabbalah is based on the Torah, I began to read the Torah regularly. I value the Torah more as a window into our tribal past than as a contract or a manual. I continue to reclaim my legacy. The display and unrolling of a Torah scroll fills me with reverence. I still have no patience for the dismal varieties of Jewish worship. Nor do I pray by addressing petitions to some sovereign power. I seek instead the elevation of consciousness within our own tradition. Emma Goldman is supposed to have said, *If I can't dance, I don't want to be part of your revolution.* And I do not need any version of Jewishness that lacks vision and joy.

E./ Tamar   30 January 2021

Looking back...Ellen aka Elana Tucker

Like many in Hashomer I grew up in a secular household. My parents met at a dance sponsored by some left-leaning group. My brother and I were Red Diaper babies though given the times it didn't get talked about. My mother's parents, immigrants from Belarus, read the Freiheit which was originally affiliated with the Communist Party. My father's parents, from Moldova, were more traditional. All of them spoke Yiddish and so did my parents to some degree. We grew up knowing we were Jewish but that wasn't a central thing in our lives. Most of our neighbors and classmates were also Jewish. We celebrated Hanukkah, and had seders at my paternal grandparents' house. What I remember is squirting seltzer across the table. One year on Rosh Hashanah, back when NYC schools didn't close, my mother made us go to school since we didn't observe the holiday. I had a good time doing art for most of the day with the three or four other kids, but wouldn't ever do that again. I did ask to go to Hebrew School, I think mostly because a bunch of my friends attended. That is when my parents began sending us to a Yiddish Shule. It was interesting, but most of the kids had been together for a while and I never felt comfortable. At some point I think I rebelled and after a year or so stopped going.

When it came to camp, my first sleep-away camp was Wel-Met run by the Jewish Federation, but I don't remember much about it. Before the next one, we spent the summer in Louisiana because my father was working there. Driving there was an eye-opening experience. Crossing the Mason-Dixon Line, seeing signs for white and colored water fountains in the supermarket or black kids waiting to get their time at the local swimming pool was something I never forgot and was something my parents had a hard time living with. Camp Woodlands was a bastion of the left. The Meeropol (Rosenberg) kids were campers. Pete Seeger came every summer and the 'Olympic Games' featured cultural programs about Cuba and Ghana as much as sports competition. Civil rights issues were front and center.

Then came Shomria summer 1962. My parents had recently bought a house and thought they would not send us to camp. Despite access to town pools it turned out Great Neck kids mostly went away to camp.They knew about Shomria through friends. I guess it was less expensive. Back then Israel had a different place in the left Jewish world so they figured learning about kibbutz and Israel was all good. Not having formed strong attachments in Great Neck, Shomria and Hashomer became a home. Weekends started with a trek into Brooklyn via train, subway and sometimes bus. The strong group culture, the discussions, the dancing, etc. became my life. I had friends at home and was part of the local teen peace movement, but Hashomer was my main thing. As I neared the end of high school I didn't want to go away to college and leave HH, which did not make my parents happy. When I wanted to go on Machon (there was not going to be a seminar) they said no. Finally, during the summer they relented if I promised to rethink the college thing and I went to Israel at the end of August 1966. To say that it was quite the year is an understatement. The first half in Jerusalem was filled with classes and travels with kids from other countries and movements. The second half on Kibbutz Revadim we worked, had some classes, made friends with kibbutznikim and I got close with my kibbutz family. We celebrated holidays in ways that gave them new meaning. That spring was the lead up to the Six Day war. It was an intense time for everyone. Friends were being called up. Revadim, I think, did not lose anyone. Afterwards we visited the place where Revadim started in Gush Etzion and then the Old City. It was both exciting but also uneasy to walk someplace where you were the conqueror. The year cemented a connection to Israel, but that has often been painful.

After a year back home, I left HH. For various reasons I wasn't going to make aliyah and unlike now, that left one no place in HH. In college there were plenty of things to get involved with: women's issues and abortion rights, anti-Vietnam War actions, etc. Not much for me on the Jewish front.

At the end of that time I met my now husband. (Hebrew played a part but that's for another time). As a friend says, every marriage is a mixed marriage even between two Jews. Though Alan did have an aunt and uncle who were part of Kfar Menachem for a bit, his was a more traditional Jewish upbringing. Israel was one connection. His grandmother made aliyah at age 75!

After fasting one year on Yom Kippur, but going to a movie with Alan and his brother, it was actually me who started us on a search for some sort of Jewish community. If I was going to fast it needed to have some meaning. When our first son was born I read a NYT article written by Paul Cowan, z'l of Village Voice fame, about a Hebrew School alternative started by parents who mostly came out of the civil rights and peace movement now wanting something Jewish for their kids. I thought, okay here is something I could live with. Apparently the parents in the early days discussed whether they should teach the ten suggestions as opposed to the ten commandments.

It is where our kids eventually landed. It met in an old synagogue, Ansche Chesed on the Upper West Side. It was a dwindling congregation being brought back to life by young people, many from the Havurah movement. There was no rabbi, it had a few employees holding the building together, and mostly functioned with volunteers taking on roles both spiritual and otherwise. It became our Jewish home. In many ways I think being part of that community filled the same needs as the movement had. Hard to believe that I now can chant Torah and I attend services. It has also been a place to engage in social justice activity. I landed up teaching at that school, the Havurah School and still do. Its focus is learning the Torah narrative, Jewish holidays and culture through the arts –storytelling, drawing, improvisation, clay, etc. Questioning encouraged.

I wonder what my Jewish life would have been without some connection to a larger community. The rhythm of life here does not revolve around the Jewish calendar as it might in Israel even if one is secular. Hashomer started that strong identification. Shabbat at moshava was a first for me. Dressing in white, white sheets and fern fronds on our cots, lighting candles, singing and dancing late into the night are powerful memories. Israeli dancing is something I came back to now quite a few years ago.

Sitting around a Shabbat or holiday table with family and friends is really more important than most moments at services.

I've been to most of the reunions, even had a few Shomrim in a class now quite a few years ago. Some things are different but I had a sense of the same kinds of connections and values HH held for them.

I've rambled on enough. These feel like difficult times both here, in Israel, and in many other places. Sad to say we are still marching and fighting for some of the same things we did back many years ago in HH or elsewhere. My mother used to talk about how she had hoped she would leave the world a better place for her children and grandchildren and sadly it wasn't in her eyes. Many days I feel the same. Looking forward to spring and hopefully seeing more people, especially my family, in person after so long. Its been great to reconnect as well.

Eric Corson, Philadelphia, PA – Eric's Thoughts and Brief History

My religious heritage is really very narrow. While my mother considered herself Jewish, it was cultural, not religious – she was an atheist. While she spoke excellent English, she did speak Yiddish with her sisters and brothers because she loved the culture of that language. She even enrolled me in a Yiddish Sunday school, though I wasn't very attracted to the school or the language. And, of course, she made sure I had a Bar Mitzvah, but it wasn't really religious because it took place at the Stephen Wise Free Synagogue – the height of liberal Judaism! I truly had no idea what I was saying or reading at the ceremony, but it was nice to have my family and friends there. The only time I went to synagogue was on Rosh Hashanah and that stopped after I was about ten. However, my mother's love for Jewish culture rubbed off on me, such as reading stories by Sholem Aleichem. And her love for nature (she was a biologist and taught biology in the New York City schools for 35 years) greatly impacted me.

I have never been attracted to religious ceremonies and actually resent someone preaching to me. It wasn't until I started relating to my half-sisters, at the age of 18, that I found a religious worship ceremony that spoke to me. My father, and his second wife, and my two sisters, were members of a Quaker Meeting in Columbus, Ohio. The first time I attended the silent Meeting for Worship, I was completely blown away – no one preaching to me, people standing up and speaking what was on their minds and, in many cases, it was about peace and justice and the horror of the Vietnam War. Eventually, I declared myself a conscientious objector and served two years of alternative service in lieu of joining the military. This took place in Columbus, where I organized a city-wide draft counseling center, a peace booth at the Ohio State Fair, and demonstrations against the war, including one where people who refused to pay their telephone tax (which was specifically created to pay for the war) gave their refused tax money to the American Friends Service Committee, the international Quaker organization. All the media covered this and I was on all the TV and radio stations and in the newspapers!

In Columbus, I also wound up visiting dozens of draft resisters who were in the local jails. That is how I learned about prison and eventually finished my alternative service and accepted the directorship of Prisoner Visitation and Support, a nationwide, interfaith visitation program for prisoners. It was through this work that I gained understanding about ecumenical religion – I worked with people from many religions: Protestants, Catholics, Jews, Muslims.

It is hard for me to be a member of any organized religion. While I am a member of a Quaker Meeting, I have never pledged allegiance to any religion. Quakers are mostly Christian, but there are some who are Jewish, Muslim and even atheist.

So, getting back to HH. Joining HH had nothing to do with my Jewishness – it was purely political, with the focus on socialism and the kibbutz – people striving to live as equals. I was not into nation states, whether it was Israel or the US. I had never been thrilled to salute and pledge allegiance to any flag, never once saluting the American flag. I remember attending a concert of the Columbus Symphony and before they began the program, they played the National Anthem and my girlfriend and I refused to stand up and someone said, "Why aren't you standing, you traitors?" Our reply was, "We'll stand when this country is worth standing up for." So, every time in HH when we were expected to salute and pledge to the Israeli flag, I had deep problems.

The most important thing about my time in HH was the people. Here were people my age who had ideals and who seemed to share an interest in forming a better world (I remember going from the Chava to the peace demonstration which surrounded the Pentagon). That is why I continue to appreciate relating to all of you. I have especially fond memories of Natan Yonatan, whose soul and poetry were so beautiful. I still have the book he wrote about losing his son, Lior, which reinforces my absolute antipathy toward war. I also note that HH was also a place where I first experienced seeing strong women of my age. This was a revelation to me.

Eric, in the middle, with Marty Braff, Ariela, Amira and Yechiel

Evelyn Goodman – My Hashomer Hatzair Experience

It was in 1962 when I was a bored high schooler that my mother found out that Hashomer Hatzair existed in Los Angeles. She had been in Hashomer in Poland before the war and had many fond memories of that time. She strongly encouraged me to check it out and after weeks of her nagging me I finally went to a Friday evening meeting. It struck me as odd with everyone wearing a blue shirt and the rituals, not to mention the Hebrew. I grew up in a secular Jewish family. After the Holocaust my parents didn't believe in a god and weren't into the religious aspects of Judaism, but they had Zionist leanings. So I was glad it wasn't a religious group. I was intrigued by it, continued to go to meetings, and before long I too was wearing a blue shirt.

I enjoyed getting to know this diverse group of people from different parts of So. California. New friendships developed. I loved the folk dancing. Discussions were stimulating and so much more interesting than what was going on in high school. Camp was fun. The difficult part of all this was the disconnection I was beginning to feel with my high school friends. They thought I had joined a weird cult and weren't interested in understanding it. While I was hurt by this, my new life within Hashomer was so much more rewarding there was no looking back.

After high school graduation I took the opportunity to go on seminar to Kibbutz Dalya for five months. This work-study immersive experience of communal life in Israel was transformative. We also had time to travel around so I was able to visit with the relatives I heard my mother talking about over the years. I loved kibbutz life, especially the young couple that became my kibbutz "parents". The hardest part of this experience was the physical labor. Getting up at 4:30 am to pick apples wasn't for me. Neither was cleaning bathrooms or working in the kitchen. So I realized that if I was going to live on a kibbutz I needed to have a more professional vocation. Whereas before I had been an unmotivated student I now looked forward to going to college and working toward a career I could do on a kibbutz. When I returned to the US I went to UC Berkeley and my participation with Hashomer ended. And, I never did go back to Israel to live on a kibbutz.

Reflecting on this now, over five decades later, it's clear to me what a pivotal role Hashomer and the seminar played in the adult I was to become. Over the years I've found it difficult to share this chapter of my life with friends because so few people can relate to it. Except for the occasional reunion of shomrim in Los Angeles it got tucked away in my history. Recently it's been lovely to reconnect periodically with several shomrim on zoom and to get to know each other now, while reminiscing about our unique Hashomer experiences. My memories for this article were triggered by these get-togethers.

Elana, Dvora (Dorothy), Rachel (Rochelle), Chava (Evelyn), Lilit (Lenor) — LA Ken

Ronit..aka Fran Marton

I grew up as an other – on the outskirts. I lived in Queens on a street that bordered a well-established middle class neighborhood, in a house behind a store that housed my father's business. My father was an immigrant who fled the then USSR in the early 1920s. I was the youngest of five, my four older siblings, a pack unto themselves, with ten years between the youngest of them and me, and a family that eschewed the materialistic lifestyle by which we were surrounded.

Although being Jewish was a part of our identity – we celebrated the notable holidays and carried the history of persecution – I found myself on the periphery of traditional Jewish culture of that time. My parents and siblings were an entity unto themselves – not affiliated with any group. We did not belong to a synagogue thus I did not attend Hebrew school nor join in the social activities with peers that were part of that milieu.

So when my mother found the ad for Camp Shomria in the back of the NY Times magazine, a six week camp for 225 dollars with a 'kibbutz-like atmosphere', she was sold and I was enrolled. And off I went at age 13 in 1958. It was there, in the movement , that I found a place to land and belong – a centered space in which I began to begin to evolve.

Hashomer Haztair provided a home where I developed a strong Jewish identity rooted in Zionism and a Weltanschauung that continues to govern a path for me.

However, after returning from Seminar on Kibbutz Dalia in 1964 and returning to Queens College I began being exposed to other experiences and people. That, coupled with a growing sense of suffocation due to the consuming time and commitment that the tnua expected/required to remain a responsible leader and member, resulted in my then making the decision to leave Hashomer Hatzair. It was most excruciating, the choice and the act. I had severed myself from a world and people where I had deep connections and a shared future. I launched myself into another sphere taking with me the values that had been inculcated by the movement. This led me into the political activities of those times, the Vietnam War, then the Women's Movement and the myriad of injustices and causes thereafter and into the present.

Israel also stayed on my radar. Its significance and spirit were housed in me. It was a destination to which I traveled many a time with family and to see family. I continue to monitor it – its politics, policies, personalities, etc. Corresponding bi-weekly for about 25 years with Yonina, formerly Frankel, has also kept me connected to the rhythm of life there.

In the interim, I married, have remained married, had a child, became a guardian for another child and now have four grandchildren. I partook in religious services on the High Holy Days for many years with my husband's family. We both did this not out of a religious belief, but out of respect for his parents – his mother, a survivor. When they died in the early 1990s this practice ended.

However, in the past several years, during this most distressing and disturbing political climate, I started to look for some perspective or grounding to assuage my escalating agitation. I was extended an invitation to a weekly Torah study group led by a female Rabbi who embraced a range of beliefs. My focus was and is to try to decipher, extrapolate, and translate the messages in the Torah into a meaning for modernity. After a year I joined the synagogue as a way of expressing and supporting Judaism. I rarely attend services, for I still spurn the concept of an almighty god, but do feel I can best enact my Jewishness and its values through Social Justice Committee's activities. The synagogue has a garden and its harvest is donated to a local organization which deals with food scarcity. Racism, Jews of Color, Jewish – Black relations, LGBQT issues are all things which are addressed. There is also a county group of which I am a member, Rockland Jews for Immigrant Justice, which supports an immigrant-led organization that provides legal services and food.

I am a clinical social worker and have worked in the mental health field for over 40 years and am still working as a psychotherapist. I feel grateful and privileged to have a profession which I love and is gratifying.

So that is my story then and now. Of course there is much in between. Relationships and values from the movement have endured and sustain an understanding that provides a sense of continuity of self and still a safe place to land.

The Old Folk Dance

The remembrance dim

a figure in a portrait

of dancing striplings.

As the music plays

a muscle memory rises

the brain maps body

movement primed decades

past. Frolicking feet abandon

body's age and aptitude..

Fran Marton

Gaby Mannheim - Hashomer Hatzair

Born in Tel Aviv at the end of WWII. Lived in a garden flat for 13 years at 133 Rechov Ben Yehuda, near Arlosarov. My parents and I emigrated from Israel in March of 1958.

My parents came from the city of Bamberg, Germany. They were engaged on Christmas Eve of 1932. My father left for Palestine at the end of February of 1933, two months after Hitler became Chancellor of Germany. My father, a Zionist, and my uncle (mother's older brother) were part of a band of Jewish retaliators operating against the local Nazis. Both felt the threat and the need to leave Germany ASAP after Hitler's rise to Chancellor. Around seven months after my father arrived in Palestine my mother arrived in Haifa. Three months later my uncle and his bride arrived, and soon after that came my mother's parents and her younger sister.

In March of 1958, we emigrated from Israel, stopping in Germany on our way to the US. In Germany, my father dealt with his family's property that was abandoned due to the Nazi government. Even though I was fluent in German, I refused to converse in German with anyone other than my parents or their friends. I recall my mother and father showing their delight in seeing the destruction of buildings in Germany. I also remember the horror in their eyes when they saw that the German police were wearing the same uniforms they had worn when my parents escaped from Germany in 1933.

We had several close entanglements with locals during our time in Germany. The luggage tags on our suitcases gave away the fact that we came from Israel, and my father was not one to back off. My father made a point of taking me to meet one person from his past. One Saturday my dad asked me to tag along with him. We went into an apartment building, knocked on one door and came face to face with this man. My father reminded him about certain events that occurred many years ago and then, looking at me, he pointed at the man and said "This is what a Nazi looks like." After three months of drudging through Germany, we arrived in the US.

We settled in Elmhurst, Queens, and I ended up attending Newtown High School. Shimon and I lived in the same apartment building and attended the same high school. At school we met and befriended Oded Tel Tzur. Oded, the son of a shaliach to Hashomer, introduced us to Hashomer. Being part of Hashomer gave me a feeling of being back with the friends I had left in Tel Aviv. Hillel was our Rosh Ken and our madrich. I recall our periods for education/discussion on Fridays and during pluga events. I enjoyed watching and listening to Chaya. She became so animated when she was addressing social issues and their merits. Chaya coached me to express my thoughts in a comfortable and coherent way. She also would correct my spoken and written English in a supportive way. During the years with Hashomer I was instilled with fundamental Jewish, socialist, and high moral values. As well as with a discipline to be inquisitive, to question, examine and work toward improving political, social and community ways. That discipline has not left me. In addition, Hashomer offered me a path to follow, in order to return to Israel.

After high school I started attending a community college, but needed to drop out and work full time. For over two years I worked for a chemical research laboratory. I needed to delay my departure to Israel, could not join my pluga's aliya, due to my role within my family. Unfortunately, I was caught up in the military draft, and ended up serving over 300 days with a combat unit in Vietnam. Fortunately, I came back whole – at least physically. During my army days, I was exposed to Jewish communities in Louisville KY, and Augusta and Savanah GA. I was flabbergasted with some of the Jewish women I met in the south. In spite of the fact that they were Jewish, they showed segregation tendencies, ignoring what our Jewish population has been exposed to in the past centuries in Europe.

Prior to the army, I never experienced any antisemitism in NYC. During the first seven months while stationed in Georgia and Kentucky I had several exposures to antisemitism. Some were very innocent. In Augusta, GA a fellow trainee from Tennessee asked one day if he could touch my head. Long story short – he was told in his community in Tennessee that Jews had horns, so he was looking for mine. We became friends after that and had several subsequent race-related conversations. When his family came to visit him, I was invited to meet the family. At the end of our training program, our training NCO invited our class to join him at a local Knights of Columbus Lodge to celebrate our completion of the course. We were dressed in our Class A army uniforms. As soon we opened the door we were stopped because two of our guys were Black. It was then my friend from Tennessee noticed the sign over the door did not welcome Jews or Blacks. We all retreated and went elsewhere. Similarly, in Kentucky, directly opposite the JCC was a private golf country club, and the sign over the entrance to the country club, specified that Jews were not allowed to enter these grounds.

I returned from Asia in late October and was assigned to an airbase in Savanah, GA. Fortunately four other fellow soldiers, with whom I had spent the previous 320 days in Asia, were also assigned to the same airbase. One fellow was married. He and his wife invited us for a Thanksgiving Dinner at their apartment. They resided in a housing rental community located away from the airbase. Us single guys, came with dates that evening. Later in the evening we all felt pretty happy and grateful for being back in the "WORLD" as we call it. As we left our friend's home, six or seven white guys were outside waiting for us. They objected that we were there, initially because one of the couples was black. My friend's wife, asked in a joking manner "How do you feel about Jews?" I do not remember their answer because a fight ensued immediately.

With the help of our dates, (once a white guy's knees buckled the women took over, manhandling them with pots, cast iron skillets etc.) we dispatched these guys to the hospital in quick order. That was our welcome back to USA.

Those 320 days in a combat zone changed us, and me in particular. In the seventies I was one of thousands of veterans camping in DC to protest against the war. For many years I seemed to have a big chip on my shoulders. My Jewishness had not changed, but the importance for returning to Israel had waned. The Zionist pull was not important to me any longer. I felt that this country, USA, now owed me something.

Upon being discharged from the army, I pursued an engineering program at SUNY Stony Brook. Several months into school, over Thanksgiving weekend, both of my parents passed. The following summer, my older sister, with her three children, and I traveled back to Israel in order to reach out to our extended family. It was a very holistic experience for all of us. During that visit I met with Shimon and Susie. If I recall correctly, I accidentally ran into Dov at an event at Heichal HaTarbut in Tel Aviv.

After completing my engineering studies, I relocated to the Boston area. It was there I met my wife-to-be at Israeli folk dancing at MIT. During the Yom Kippur War I was involved in soliciting public support for the Israeli war effort. At this effort I saw and met with Judy and Tzvi Body.

My wife and I have three children and we currently reside in Chicago. We joined a Chicago Reform Temple, predominately to expose our children to the Jewish community, history, and tradition. We hoped the process would help us instill a Jewish identity in them. My Jewish identity was born into me in Israel. My wife's Jewish identity has grown by her family participation in their temple. I believe our efforts have succeeded. The degree of Jewishness which has manifested, is different in each of them. Two of them went on a birthright trip. Our oldest son spent his junior college year in Israel studying at the Hebrew University in Jerusalem. His experience in Israel opened his eyes to consider more than just one side of issues in that part of the world. It also established a fluency with the Hebrew language. He shared his experience with his siblings. All three are very comfortable with their Jewishness and are progressive in their views about society issues, equality with their peers, and accepting of new adventures.

My value system and moral compass were not abandoned since my active years with Hashomer. Some may have been bent a bit while serving in the US Army, but not broken. I truly cherish and honor my Hashomer experience. My recent viewing of a picture of young Jewish Holocaust Survivors with a Chazak V'Ematz banner, along with their resolve to leave for Palestine, has refreshed my gratefulness to have been part of the Hashomer movement.

Shimon, Elana, Shoshana and Gaby

"A few seconds before taking this picture a beluga whale shot a mouth full of water at me."

Guy Koretz (Ken Negba in Detroit, Gal-On & Jerusalem)

End of February?! Guess I better get my tachat in gear. Actually I don't have a whole lot to say. My values, Jewish and in general, weren't much affected by HH. I was attracted to the movement by its collectivist and pro-Israel sentiments.

I felt at home with those ideals. What changed for me was my identity. I identify more as Israeli than Jewish. Of course there is plenty of overlap. I think being in Tzahal and the War of Attrition played a significant part in that. When I finally "settled down" it was in Utah because Salt Lake City is my late wife's home town.

I really love the wide open spaces (ten times the size of Israel), the mountains, the desert, the snow, red rock country, the national parks and monuments.

The Mormons love Israel and are impressed by my Israeliness. Their Tanach (Book of Mormon) is about people who left Israel to come to America. It's pretty tedious, the musical is more entertaining. Their main school (Brigham Young University) maintains a study center in Jerusalem, the father of one of my best friends here was the director there for a year and a half.

Personal connections I made in the movement mean more to me than Socialism, Zionism or any of that other stuff. When I heard that Zoie died I happened to be on Prince Edward Island. I went to St. Dunstan's Cathedral in Charlottetown and lit one of those votive candles in his memory. Not a very Jewish thing to do, is it? I hadn't seen him in 45 years and even when we were on seminar and living in Jerusalem at the same time I didn't hang out with him much. Still I felt a need to grieve the loss. I generally still identify with the values and ideas I held in the movement but the personal connections I made with people are what I treasure the most.

Guy in 1979 in the Bay Area

Hillel Schenker, has lived in Tel Aviv since 1985, was in Hashomer Hatzair from 1952-1963, and on a Hashomer kibbutz, Barkai from 1963 till 1976, co-editor of the Jerusalem-based Palestine-Israel Journal (www.pij.org) since 2002.

I have a rather unique background, having been born in a movement urban kibbutz in Brooklyn during WW II, and the first language I heard there was Hebrew, so I can say that's my "mother tongue" though I have naturally no memories of that. As a child, I almost never went to a synagogue, though I do remember once going on Purim and shaking a "groger" noisemaker every time Haman's name was read. I remember that during Friday night family dinners, candles were lit, until one day they disappeared. I had a bar mitzvah, mainly because I knew it was important for my grandfather, and I insisted that my haftorah teacher make a record so I could memorize it the way I memorized all the early rock and roll songs. That was also probably the last time I put on tefillin (Google says the English word for that is phylacteries). The primary traditional Jewish custom that I celebrated with my family throughout my childhood and youth was the Pesach seder, one with each side of the family. And on Chanukah, we placed a chanukiya in the window and lit the candles like all the other Jews in the very Jewish neighborhoods I lived in. And we sang "I have a little dreidel", "Oh Chanukah oh Chanukah Come Light My Menorah" and some Hebrew songs. We also dipped apple slices in honey on Rosh Hashana.

As for any antisemitism in my youth, here I have to quote Mel Brooks (aka Melvin Kaminsky) in an interview he gave to a very staid guy from the BBC who asked whether he had suffered any antisemitism in his childhood. He responded, "anti-Semitism? In Brooklyn? Not possible, everyone was Jewish!" The Syrians did fire at me and my IDF "comrades" when I was serving for seven months on the Golan Heights during the Yom Kippur War in 73/74, but that was not because they were anti-Semites who had read "The Protocols of the Elders of Zion", but rather because they wanted to get the Heights back. That extended war-time experience on the front lines changed my priorities from music and thoughts of a possible academic career to a focus on engaged journalism/peace activism.

I also had no direct connection with the Holocaust when I was growing up, since my parents were born in the States and everyone around me was a 3rd generation American Jew. I first met Holocaust survivors only when I arrived on Kibbutz Barkai which was founded by Polish and Romanian Holocaust survivors, some of whom had been in concentration camps. I was totally opposed to anything German until I met the first German volunteers who came to the kibbutz in the summer of 1967 after the war to help out. https://www.pij.org/articles/1973/an-israelis-thoughts-about-germans- and-palestinians. I then began to meet young Germans in the anti-nuclear movement in Europe, and eventually visited Germany and Berlin for the first time in 2009 on the 20th anniversary of the fall of the Berlin Wall. Today I greatly appreciate the fact that the German political foundations are among the primary funders and supporters of the Israeli peace movement and have a very good working relationship with them, particularly with the representatives of the Friedrich Ebert Foundation (connected to the SPD – Social Democratic Party).

Being in Hashomer Hatzair in New York from the age of nine till 21 clearly added additional dimensions to my Jewish identity. The kibbutz-style third seder, based on the kibbutz Hagadah, added a modern Israeli dimension to the way the holiday was celebrated, which incorporated elements of spring, liberation, freedom and peace into the festivities. By the time I reached high school, my primary social framework was the friends in the movement. Many of the people in my shichva also went to Marshalia Hebrew High School on Tuesday and Thursday afternoons in Brooklyn and the Bronx (Ami Sperber, Zvi Body, Malka Tuchman, Amira Broder, Peretz Goldblatt), We would all meet together on Sundays in Manhattan, so a Hebrew, biblical and historical education was added to the dimension of my, and I assume, our Jewish identities, which included Hebrew songs and dances, which we also did in the movement, and of course at moshava.

This was reinforced with a year of the machon experience, the Institute for Youth Leaders from Abroad, a half year of intensive study in Jerusalem and a half year on Kibbutz Shoval, where our teacher was Yehuda Bauer, who eventually went on to become a prominent professor at Hebrew U. of Holocaust Studies and senior consultant at the Yad Va'shem Holocaust Memorial.

The Hashomer Hatzair youth movement and machon experiences were amplified by the experience of living on a Hashomer kibbutz for 13 years. There, a celebration of Chag Habikurim, Tu B'shvat and Purim were additional communal holiday highlights added to my Jewish identity calendar, alongside Yom Ha'atzmaut (Independence Day), Yom Hashoah (Holocaust Day), Yom Hazikaron (Memorial Day) and...May 1, all perhaps more Israeli national and international, rather than strictly Jewish. The other element was the focus on Hebrew, the revived modernized biblical language as the language of communication. Despite the fact that a majority of the members came from English-speaking countries, there was a principle of speaking only Hebrew in the public sphere. Of course, there was also the Friday night communal Oneg Shabbat, the weekly secular celebration which replaced the traditional religious Friday night at a synagogue.

I left the kibbutz in 1976, not because I had become disillusioned with the way of life but because of personal circumstances. After moving to the city, and eventually to Tel Aviv where I have been living since 1985, I now live a block away from the home, now museum, of Bialik, the Israeli national poet, where on Friday evenings he used to host a secular Oneg Shabbat focusing on culture, literature and music. When Mickey Gitzin, now the executive director of the New Israel Fund in Israel, was serving as head of the Cultural Department in the Tel Aviv Municipality, he initiated a modern version of Bialik's Oneg Shabbat, always held on Saturdays, beginning with a reading of the weekly Torah portion with a modern interpretation, with the centerpiece being a singer, musical troupe or literary figure. Although he grew up in a right-wing Russian-Jewish family, and obviously was not in Hashomer Hatzair, he moved to the left after being exposed to alternative lifestyles and approaches during his studies in the U.S. and the UK, and was a representative of the left-Zionist Meretz on the City Council. I went regularly, particularly when it was held at the Municipal Music Library on Bialik Square, a block away from my apartment. I also went pretty regularly (in the pre-Corona era) to the Thursday evening literary evenings at Bialik House, built around either a literary theme or writer, always with an appropriate musical interlude at the beginning, middle and end. All of these events, along with the neighborhood café culture and the ongoing contact with fellow peace activists clearly provide a sense of community that one may get also from a congregation or chavurah. Perhaps if I lived in the States I would feel the need to be part of a liberal/progressive congregation or chavurah, for the sake of being part of a Jewish community. Here I don't feel that need to realize a sense of belonging to a community.

If the Christians have their trinity of the Father, the Son and the Holy Ghost (though Jesus was Jewish throughout his life), then I always thought, inspired by the principles of Hashomer Hatzair, that the Jewish trinity was Marx, Einstein and Freud. I would later add Martin Buber, who had a major influence on the thought and philosophy of Hashomer Hatzair. His emphasis on the importance of dialogue, "I & Thou" in the relationship of man to man, man to woman, nation to nation and man and his God, has been one of the guiding principles of my engaged journalism/activism at New Outlook, where Buber was the direct inspiration, and now at the Palestine-Israel Journal (www.pij.org), whose very essence is dialogue. In general, I identify being Jewish with what is defined in the States as being active in the struggle for Tikkun Olam, repairing the world, and in Israel as Tzedek Chevrati, social justice.

Speaking of God, while I respect people who believe, as long as they don't try to impose their beliefs and customs on others, or distort things along the lines of Dylan's "With God on Our Side" https://genius.com/Bob-dylan-with-god-on-our-side-lyrics, personally, my view has always been that God is an invention of man to help explain the nature of life and the universe. I particularly admire Jews and non-Jews who channel their belief systems into some form of liberation theology. And I know at least two graduates of Hashomer Hatzair who became rabbis, Rain Zohav and Amita Jarmon, who very much practice what they preach. So I am a secular Jew, an atheist, though I would prefer to put it in the positive, not the absence of something, but the positive, a humanistic Jew.

It's worth noting that today, according to recent studies, people living in Israel whose primary self-definition is being Jewish tend to be on the right, while people whose primary self-definition is being an Israeli tend to be on the left.

So yes, I am an Israeli (who also holds American citizenship), and I am a secular Jew, who believes in the Jewish right to national self-determination, alongside the equal Palestinian right to national self-determination. I see that combination as the fulfillment of the ideals and spirit contained in the experience of having been a member of Hashomer Hatzair.

Hillel, seated, playing guitar

Joan/Nechama Price/Rahav

My first year at Camp Shomria I was 11 years old. I discovered the movement exactly on the brink of my becoming a teenager. I needed to get out of the house, to find new horizons, and to make new friends.

After camp there was the Bronx Ken and Ami Sperber. That first year I determined that Hashomer Hatzair was my whole life. It gave me an identity. I was embraced, and I embraced back. It gave me perspective on life. It gave me a third dimension in the two dimensional world I was in. This was invaluable. My new friends were the dearest thing to me. The intensity of my involvement escalated. I really loved the movement. Now, 60 years later, I can articulate that I have a strong attraction to spirituality and idealism. I always wish for something to believe in. In those years the movement met my need. I believed. I loved. I wanted to devote my life to going to Israel, and drying swamps, and dancing the hora all night, and being a halutz.

Life intervened and my poor, blessed, mother got very sick. I left the New York movement and my friends in the Bronx Ken and went to Israel when I was 15. I missed out on being a madricha and navigating the more adult aspects of being in Hashomer. I arrived in Israel. This was a similar experience to having gone to the movies and being swept up in some fabulous cinematic experience and then, having the harsh lights at the end of the movie go on. Looking around, you see that there are candy wrappers on the floor and gum stuck to the chair in front of you and the floor is scuzzy and the people around you are not glamorous, and going to the restroom the people in line are loudmouthed, and bang! poof! pop! the illusion ended. Reality kicked in. Don't get me wrong. The people on the kibbutz were lovely. They were good people, and kind to me. My fevered imagination wasn't prepared for reality however. Nobody danced the hora all night. There were no swamps to be dried. It was plain and simple the banality of everyday life. This was not a spiritually charged existence. I was crushed. I didn't identify with it. Also, hey, I was an American immigrant girl. People made fun of my American accent. I didn't speak Hebrew yet (eventually of course I did). People made fun of me, people made fun of my clothes. I had left behind everything I knew. My dear old friends in the movement were gone from my life, at that moment.

My crash landing onto reality put me in the position of wanting to search for something new to believe in. I couldn't believe in kibbutz anymore, because nobody that was already there believed in it. Everybody was just living their life day to day, no ideology at all.

I found a book at this juncture, when I didn't know what to do next. I found a book because I am a bookworm. I love books, I always find a book. I found a book called "My Life in Art" by Stanislavski. This book describes how you devote yourself to the theater. I determined I would get out of the kibbutz (indeed I did) and I would devote myself to art. This I did. I left the kibbutz and devoted myself to theater for five years. The same experience played out. I dreamt of imagined glory, and then when I faced reality, reality was stark and did not match my imagination. My third quest took me to Tel Aviv University. I began to study economics. Then life took over, I got married etc. etc.

Did Hashomer give me my political identity? Did Hashomer give me my Jewish identity? Somewhat. My Jewish identity was strongly influenced by encountering Zionism. It did shift my entire life. Certainly I would never have gone to Israel without Dov Zakin and Amos Ben Israel mentoring and arranging it. I do not know where I would have wound up otherwise. Perhaps with no Jewishness in me at all. I do not see my political identity as having been directly guided by my movement years. I went to a very left-wing kibbutz and studied Marxism. Then I went to Tel Aviv University and studied economics. My political views are formed by those experiences. I tend to be pragmatic. I view myself as a pragmatic economist and I view the political leanings of Hashomer Hatzair as wishful thinking more than a possible course of action. In any case I am not a political activist in my heart. I am very involved with business and economics and art and theatre, and the creative process. I am not really a political animal.

The formative years I spent in the movement certainly shaped and re-shaped my life, however. It is with tremendous tenderness and poignant nostalgia that I embrace our group reconnecting and sharing, in these lovely remote virtual meetings.

Some Things Don't Change - Joey Beinin

My father and two uncles were leaders of Hashomer Hatzair in New York. Both my parents were members of the garin that established Kibbutz Sasa. They lived in Palestine during the last years of the British Mandate, but never joined the kibbutz. My mother worked in the secretarial pool at Consolidated Refineries in Haifa, where most of her co-workers were Palestinian Arab women.

In those days Hashomer Hatzair supported a bi-national state. My mother repeatedly told me, as I was growing up, about her warm relations with her Arab co-workers. On December 30, 1947, the Etzel threw bombs at Arab workers waiting at the main gate of the refinery to be hired, destroying the good Arab-Jewish relations that had previously prevailed. My mother cursed Menachem Begin for this for the rest of her life. My former chanich and close friend and collaborator, Zach Lockman, has written a good account of these events. Ami Isseroff's (z"l) edited version of Zach's narrative is at this link - http://www.mideastweb.org/refriots.htm.

My parents returned to the US before the State of Israel was established because my father had been badly wounded in the Battle of the Bulge in World War II and couldn't fight in another war. PTSD was not well understood then.

I was born in South Philadelphia. We lived in the home of my maternal grandparents, who spoke little English, until I was four and a half. The main language of the home and the neighborhood was Yiddish. So with my parents' experiences in Hashomer Hatzair and Palestine and growing up speaking Yiddish, I had a secular, left-wing Zionist, Jewish identity before I knew what an identity was.

When my family moved to northeast Philadelphia, as many upwardly mobile Jewish families did, regular antisemitism at school and on the playground seared that identity into my heart. My parents were anti-religious in the style of the Israeli League for the Prevention of Religious Coercion of the 1950s. Nonetheless, they joined Conservative synagogues and supported my taking off from school and going to synagogue on every Jewish holiday and every Shabbat. I had a traditional Bar Mitzvah. I still know many of the prayers and Torah verses by heart.

I first went to Camp Shomria in Liberty for Mosh Construction in 1958, when my father (Benzion, z"l) and uncle (Duddy, z"l) helped build the first tzrifim of the Machaneh Kovshim. I returned the next year for my first full summer at Shomria. It took me about two weeks after arriving to decide (at the ripe age of ten) that I was going to live in Israel on a kibbutz.

We lived in Philadelphia so I could not go to ken meetings, although I continued to go to Camp Shomria every year except one. My family moved to Metuchen, NJ when I was 15. But I had almost no engagement with Metuchen. Between Hebrew high school and the movement, I was in the City five days a week.

The movement became the center of my social, cultural, and intellectual life. We created a subculture that nurtured us, drawing on both the traditions of Hashomer Hatzair (minus the Stalinism of the 1940s and early 1950s) and the contemporary American new left. We cared deeply and bonded to each other despite the inevitable frictions. We read poetry. We went to museums. We discovered the city. The boys played tackle football without protective equipment in Central Park. Everyone else played touch. We were crazy!

In 1965-66 I went on the seminar le-madrichim at Kibbutz Gal-On and Mishmar Ha-Emek. I loved the seminar. At Gal-On, Ariel Hurwitz taught me to milk cows, and I worked in the refet. When we moved to Mishmar Ha-Emek after a month, I again worked in the refet. The regular raftanim gave me lots of responsibilities. Driving around in a tractor and milking 250 cows alone on Shabbat was heady stuff for a 16-17 year-old and gave me self-confidence and competence beyond my years. I also loved the seminar because Miriam (and Lilit Schatzberg and Naomi Schenker z"l) were my roommates.

After 12 years of Hebrew school, my Hebrew was reasonably good. So, at Mishmar Ha-Emek I asked if, instead of participating in Hebrew classes, they could teach me Arabic. Our madrichim readily agreed. I began studying with Rachamim (z"l), the Arabic teacher of the Mossad Chinuchi. He had been a member of the Iraqi youth aliya group on the kibbutz, which is the subject of Eli Amir's novel, *Tarnigol Kaparot* (translated into English as "Scapegoat").

My first conversation in Arabic with an Arab was when I accompanied Rachamim on home visits in Umm al-Fahm to convince Palestinians who worked on neighboring Hashomer Hatzair kibbutzim to vote for Mapam in the 1966 elections. There are many things wrong with that picture. But I've written about it elsewhere.

Meeting your future wife, madrichim putting chocolate on our pillows every Shabbat, educational discussions with members of the Knesset (there were two on the kibbutz as well as Ya'akov Chazan, a leader of Mapam), Rachel Manor (a pioneer of kibbutz-style collective education), and others, beginning to learn Arabic, and engagement in Israeli politics (before I understood what was up): My experiences at Mishmar Ha-Emek were quintessentially Hashomer Hatzair – a unique amalgam of emotionally intense collective life, intellectual exploration, eroticism, and what I then believed was socialist internationalism.

Returning from seminar, I became a madrich in the Queens ken and eventually rosh ken. To be a good madrich I had to learn many things that were esoteric knowledge at Princeton University, where I was studying for a BA in Near East Studies (although my academic advisor, Avraham Udovitch, had belonged to Hashomer Hatzair in Winnipeg). Along with several other college students in the movement, I argued about Zionism with anti-Zionists in the New Left. We also argued with the shlichim who did not want us to wear chultzot shomriot at demonstrations against the Vietnam War. Very likely, they were concerned that protesting the war would instill in us an anti-militarist spirit; for much of my shichva, they were correct.

Members of my shichva went to the chavat hachshara in the spring of 1969, when I was in my junior year at Princeton. There, I got up at 5am to milk our 32 cows with Linda Rubin before heading off to my Arabic class and returned in time for the afternoon milking. I am eternally grateful to Elana Michaelson for writing the final paper for my comparative literature class. I could not have managed it under those circumstances.

During the summer before we decided to close the chava, I attended an intensive Arabic course at the American University in Cairo. There, I met Palestinian students who introduced me to PLO members, some of whom had been trained in China and Algeria. This was disorienting for someone who identified with the anti-imperialist left. In the late 1960s and 1970s, the standard Zionist position was that asserting that there was a Palestinian people was simply antisemitism. After returning from Cairo I spoke to the older members of the movement about my experiences there (at the mo'adon merkaz, for those who remember that term). I didn't have a clear political position. I only knew that the Palestinian students I met were not anti-Semites and that they were Palestinians, not generic Arabs. Several shlichim were unhappy that I felt sure about this much.

In September 1970 Miriam and I joined our garin at Kibbutz Lahav, which was the polar opposite of Mishmar Ha-Emek, even discounting for my idealized memory of it. Before a year was up we decamped for Jerusalem. I began studying for my MA in History of the Islamic Countries at the Hebrew University. In the milieu of the Israeli New Left (Siach), I began to reconsider everything I had learned and taught others in Hashomer Hatzair. My mentor in that process was the late Reuven Kaminer (z"l), a graduate of the Detroit ken who left us last Rosh Hashanah. My obituary for him is at this link - https://www.972mag.com/reuven-kaminer-israel-radical-left/.

After some detours, including working in an auto factory in Detroit and political organizing among Arabs (mainly Yemenis and Palestinians) in Dearborn, I began an academic career. For 35 years I taught modern Middle East history at Stanford University (with a two-year break at the American University in Cairo).

Arriving at Stanford in 1983 with a strong critique of Israel's 1982 invasion of Lebanon meant it was not possible to find a place in the provincial Jewish community of the San Francisco Peninsula.

CODA

I retired from Stanford in 2019, and we moved to Portland, Oregon full time to be close to our family members. We joined Havurah Shalom, a progressive Reconstructionist synagogue, where I teach adult education courses on Israel/Palestine, Jews of the Middle East and North Africa, and related topics. So, after decades of having been alienated from the mainstream institutional American Jewish community, I've reconnected in an unexpected but very familiar way.

Kibbutz Lahav raised (and still raises) pigs. We and our Israeli friends used to go to East Jerusalem to buy pork chops from Christian Arab butchers to eat on Yom Kippur. I still eat pork, as does my brother's family who live on Kibbutz Shomrat and Nir Oz (My sister, who lives in Givatayim, is vegan, so out of the game). Hebrew-speaking, left-wing, secular, pork-eating Jews is what we were raised to be. I still am.

Joey Beinin

February 2021

Miriam Beinin, Donnie Goldstein, Joey Appel and Joey Beinin

Laura MacAlevey (Laurie Weinstein), social worker, retired, United Kingdom

My introduction to HH was incidental, or perhaps better described as serendipitous. Little did my parents know what impact it would have on my life when, at age 13, my parents went off to Europe on vacation and shipped me off to Camp Shomria. They must have read the literature which included the words 'secular, Jewish and humanistic.' I had received very little education about the Jewish religion as my parents were atheists and although we celebrated the usual Jewish festivals, we never went to synagogue except for weddings, funerals and my brother's Bar Mitzvah, undertaken in respect of my grandmother. They had been Trotskyite activists in their youth who had met on soap boxes, but by the time I came along, they were armchair radicals (like I suppose I am also now).

Growing up during the McCarthy period, my father informed me at a young age that the US government was monitoring our telephone and mail due to his past political activities. This not only made me anxious, but set me up for feeling alienated from the country of my birth, though I always felt proud of my unconventional upbringing. I was taken to classical music concerts and art museums and book shelves lined our walls. My father was a writer and book publisher from whom I inherited my love of the written word and also my socialist realism/skepticism about anything that couldn't be proven. No teeth under the pillow for the tooth fairy, no Disney. I realised that there were different kinds of Jews, who were equally Jewish, but in different ways. My parents were not Zionists but shortly before I went on aliya, my father gave me a book about Judaism. He inscribed on the front page that he was 'in wonderment and delight at my Jewish mind and spirit', the book's title.

I was already an idealist looking for a cause when I went to Camp Shomria. In HH, I was offered an alternative community of people who were hopeful and positive about building a better society in Israel and on kibbutz. I loved the singing, dancing and the camaraderie and by the end of camp, I was smitten. I have very fond memories of those years as a teenager, going to the ken every week and I proceeded through the stages to seminar, the chava and finally aliya. I never doubted my path and defended it vigorously. I became a madricha in my local ken, my first experience of working with children which turned into a lifelong career. As I progressed through the different tiers of the tnua, we met up with chaverim from other parts of NYC and other cities. I became aware that HH was a world wide community of people like ourselves and that it had started in Europe before the State of Israel was founded – those early Socialist Zionists were our heroes.

We had many shlichim who came from different kibbutzim in Israel. Natan Yonatan was the shaliach of our ken and also of our shichva. My first Hebrew teacher on seminar gave me a book of his poems in Hebrew, as she wanted me to keep up my study of Hebrew back home. I kept that book and have recently looked Natan up on You Tube and found videos of him as an old man. I heard him speak in his familiar dulcet voice at various commemorations of his extensive literary works, along with hearing many of the familiar songs his lyrics were set to, with some very beautiful Russian melodies that I still recognise and can sing along with.

It is impossible to put my memories and the influence of HH in any semblance of order, either chronologically or geographically. Memories blur over time and as a Jew of three different countries on three different continents, my experience and memories are interwoven into my contemporary life in magical and mysterious ways. As a young child, I first recognised the phenomenon of antisemitism when we were traveling on vacation and stopped in a diner in a small town. I ordered an open hot roast beef sandwich which arrived on the table with a green tinge. My aunt thought that they had served us this because we looked Jewish! So as we left, she poured salt into the jam and jam into the sugar! I was baffled. Ten years later when a group of neo-Nazis were having a rally in New York City, a group of us from HH went to demonstrate against them. I hadn't known much about the Holocaust growing up, as they did not discuss it at school and my immediate family was not affected personally. My grandparents were safe in the US by then, having emigrated from Russia in the early 1900s. The story goes that they were escaping the pogroms and landed on Ellis Island. Fearful they would be traced by the Czar, they asked the immigration official to open the Bronx phone book and choose a popular Jewish name. Actually, it was my living amongst Holocaust survivors and their children on the kibbutz and also my living in Europe all these years that has enlightened me to really understand the effects of the Holocaust on Jewish consciousness and my own.

When we went on seminar in 1965, we were allocated kibbutz families and I learned Hebrew very quickly. When I returned to Gal-On some 30 years after I had left the kibbutz, when I entered the dining room, a woman approached me and said that she remembered my making batik and hanging it out on a washing line to dry. She had been nine at the time, demonstrating that WE also had an effect on the kibbutz! I remained in touch with my kibbutz friends and my kibbutz family when we came back from seminar and when the Six Day War broke out, I flew to Gal-On to help out on the kibbutz for the summer. I started college the year after that, but left to go to the chava which dismayed my parents, but I insisted that college would not help further my life on kibbutz. I enjoyed my time at the chava, doing manual labour and the cultural and social life we enjoyed. I also learned that living communally might mean that the bicycle I had brought with me was now communal property! There was definitely a culture clash between trying to live communally and how we had grown up, each in our individual families. When I filled out embarkation forms on the boat we took to Israel, instructed to write down our profession, I wrote PIONEER.

I lived happily on the kibbutz for three or four more years, working in a gan yeladim, but then got itchy feet and decided I wanted to go to university. When I finished my degree in Special Education and Counselling, I had been in Aretz for five years and my immigration and tax rights were ending which meant I had to quickly buy everything I needed to set up home. I was not ready for that at the tender age of 23, so decided to leave Israel for a year so that my immigrant rights would start again on my return. However, I never did return and that was mainly because outside Israel, I realized how stressed I felt with the security situation which nothing we had learned in HH could have prepared me for. Israel was only 20 years old then and I had already experienced being there soon after a war and another one followed a few years later. And then others. I had to take my security anxieties in my stride when I lived there, but when I left, I recognised that a burden had been lifted from me.

I spent a few years back in the US where I did my Masters degree in Social Work and then was offered a job in England where I have lived since 1976. I didn't visit Israel for many years after coming to England, at first because I was missing it so much and regretted leaving. I knew that going back to visit was going to be difficult for me. In later years, I felt uncomfortable with the direction of Israeli politics. I couldn't cope with the right wing swing, the ever expanding settlements, the power of the ultra religious minority as well as the privatisation of kibbutz. Frequently dreams would haunt me about my youth and young adulthood in Israel and when I reached sixty, I knew that I had to make my peace. After all, I still visited the US whose politics I abhorred. I didn't want to come home after these visits as I was so warmly welcomed. On one visit I rented a room on the kibbutz for two months. However, when I did visit, I found it very hard to keep my opinions to myself with friends who were living the reality and of whom I was so very fond. Their outlooks had changed whilst mine were stuck in an old groove.

My Jewish identity has actually become stronger living in Europe, although married to a non-Jew and having non-Jewish adopted children was a challenge. My husband could not understand my strong Jewish identity and pride, as he himself was traumatised by his Catholic boarding school and by the Church. Most non-Jews have difficulty understanding that we Jews have a tribe mentality, i.e. Judaism is not just a religion, although in Britain the secular Jewish culture is not nearly as strong as it was in the U.S. As far as the humanist element, here in Britain, I found that socialism was not a dirty word and still isn't, though this is a very different Britain than the one I found when I first arrived. Year by year, we catch up with the US in greed and privatisation of public services and the rich and powerful and multi-national companies still influence the laws. However, there remains an ethos in Britain that does not exist in the U.S. and although 'from cradle to grave' is no longer the motto of Social Services, the NHS remains a national treasure as do the many international and local charities that support vulnerable populations both here and abroad. Fund raising and charity work are national pastimes and charity shops proliferate. Extreme right-wing and racist ideology is not tolerated, as it is in the U.S.

Spoiled for an individualistic life by my experience of kibbutz and craving a feeling of belonging, I have since always sought a sense of community. I found it in different guises over the years, at first in the socialist feminist movement of 70s London and then in a bio-energetic therapeutic network which lasted many years. Many of us moved to the countryside to be near each other and we had a rich social and community life, not dissimilar to what I enjoyed in HH, though centered on becoming emotionally healthier within ourselves, with other people and in the world. Among us, as in many 'alternative communities' there were always Jews. My husband and I got married in a registry office, but I composed my own Jewish marriage ceremony for afterwards which my Jewish and non-Jewish friends helped me write and organise which took place under a chupa that I had sewn myself. Under my beautiful chupa, we recited our vows and my husband Mike broke the glass cup with extreme fervour. There was dancing and singing. The village we lived in was also very progressive and had a Steiner/Waldorf school as well as several related colleges which attracted many Israelis, some of whom became friends. I could recognise an Israeli accent a mile off and had the chance to speak Hebrew often. Likewise, when I traveled and heard fellow tourists speaking Hebrew, it felt like a reminder of "home".

In the vibrant multi-cultural city of nearby Brighton, which boasts the only Green Party MP in the UK, a university, a large community of Jews as well as being the gay capitol of Britain (they call it London by the sea!), I found a network of liberal feminist Jewish women. Many of us have a strong connection to Israel, including Israelis living here and others whose children, grandchildren or they themselves have lived or still live in Israel. It was at this group that I met a South African woman who grew up in HH in South Africa and whose experiences and memories are almost identical to my own. The group has a communal seder, latkes evenings over Chanukah and groups for sharing experiences. There is a also a Jewish Community Centre where films on Jewish themes and Israeli films are screened monthly. On the major anniversaries of the State of Israel, there have been huge gatherings with Israeli food and dancing. I am always reminded of the risk of anti Semitic attacks by the close monitoring of guests and the presence of security guards from the dedicated Jewish security organisation that travels all over the country to protect large public Jewish events. Although there are several synagogues and one progressive one in Brighton, the religious aspect of Judaism is still very foreign to me.

There is growing antisemitism from the right in Europe, but from my experience, antisemitism is not tolerated, either by the British government (whatever persuasion) or the public in Britain. I myself have never experienced direct antisemitism in my 45 years here, although I have experienced quite a bit of anti-Americanism. Living in a Christian country as a Jew, there are many compromises to be made. My daughter was chosen to play Mary in the school Christmas play and I had no desire to refuse this. In her Waldorf nursery, there was continual talk on holidays of the 'Christ Child' which alienated me. Nonetheless, I have been in several choral societies singing Christian music, just for the love of the music. I have created beautiful Nativity figures to sell for the love of fabric crafts. I do send Christmas cards, but only buy or make cards that say PEACE ON EARTH. I feel like an expat in all my three countries and I criticise them all equally, whilst also recognising the good things in each. There is a left-wing anti Israel contingent here and as everywhere, the line between antisemitism and criticising Israel is a fine one. As a progressive Jew I am also against Israel's expansionist policies, the treatment of Palestinians and the Occupation and watching the tragedies in Gaza, does raise conflicts in my heart and mind that I cannot resolve. I do however remain a firm believer in the need for a Jewish state, so I suppose I am still a Zionist at heart.

In the UK, the history of World War II and the Holocaust is much closer to the general population as it took place on our doorstep. I remember my children, even in primary school, putting on plays about the war and making gas masks. There are many WWII commemorations throughout the year here and across Europe. The soldiers who fought are becoming fewer and fewer, as are the survivors of the Holocaust. Nicholas Winton who rescued hundreds of Jewish children from the camps and transported them to England in the Kinder Transport is revered. Recently I watched a video of a reunion with him and the elderly survivors, meeting for the first time. It was moving beyond words, with tears on all sides. Holocaust Memorial Day is widely commemorated and the concept of 'lest we forget' is very strong here and in many other Western European countries.

I like to travel and attended Rosh Ha Shana in the last remaining synagogue in Sarajevo, also attended by a coachload of Israeli tourists. I was also at a public ceremony recognising the place of Jews in the ancient port city of Essaouira on the Moroccan coast. I sought and found old Jewish quarters and museums in Thessaloniki, Bulgaria, Croatia, Vienna, Italy and Spain and I met many Israelis and Jews from around the world following my same tracks. I also encountered Holocaust denial amongst some Eastern Europeans which was distressing.

I have always kept my memories of HH and life on kibbutz and Israel alive. I still do Israeli folk dancing and can still carry out a decent conversation in Hebrew, though I now struggle sometimes to find words in English, oddly, they come to me more easily in Hebrew. As I am a bit of a polyglot and can speak basic Italian, Spanish and French, they often get confused in my mind with Hebrew. One of my friends from kibbutz asked me to buy some batteries for her mobile phone when I was last visiting. I could not remember the Hebrew word for batteries, but the work 'pil' came to mind from French or Spanish, which I then pluralised and asked in the shop for 'pilim', which is 'elephants' in Hebrew!

During Covid, the reawakening of old memories and reconnection with old HH friends has been a blessing, but also sad at times. We each have our own individual memories and experiences from the tnua, from kibbutz, from Israel and from our lives as Jews in the Diaspora, but It is clear to me that HH has been a major weft in the tapestry of all of our lives and where it all started for many of us.

Ira Orenstein, Joey Beinin, Laura, Artie
(Yehuda) Blumberg and Meri

Clockwise - Laura, Yehuda, Teddy
(Theo) Vermont, Marty Braff

Laura, in front, is second from right

95

Laura aka Lilit Schatzberg – Bronx, NY/Point Arena, CA

It is not surprising that so many of us came from families that were secular and left-leaning. After all, who would a socialist-zionist youth movement attract? I would never have encountered Hashomer Hatzair if my cousin had not pointed me in its direction.

My mother was born in Jerusalem and immigrated to the US when she was 12. Her father and two brothers came here before. Her father was an artist at Betzalel in Jerusalem and first came to learn techniques for his work as a 'tzoref', an engraver. He had a brother in NYC and for reasons I do not know but can speculate on, he decided to bring the rest of the family and not return to Palestine just yet. My father was a first generation son from parents from Bulgaria and Ukraine – then Poland and the Pale of Settlement. I know little about their background but they were not religious as far as I knew. My mother's parents were not either. My mother did tell stories about her religious maternal grandmother but she stayed behind in Jerusalem and I think she died soon after they left. My father spoke no Hebrew but he and my mother had enough Yiddish to occasionally use it to tell secrets. My mother's older sister and her family returned to Israel after statehood was declared. My grandparents followed soon after when I was about nine months old. With her brothers and other friends and relatives my mother spoke Hebrew so I heard it my whole life. At times I would ask her to teach me but it never happened. Having stopped learning it at 12 I think she did not feel up to the task. I only began to learn when I was on seminar in 1965-66. It came quite easily to me and I enjoyed being able to communicate in it with relatives. Though I have not lived in Israel for years I still use it though it is a bit rusty and I am not up on the current slang.

For as long as family remained on the East Coast we had holidays together. The content of these celebrations was minimal but the good feelings, fun, and food were nurturing and nourishing. My aunt and uncle learned some folk dances and we would all dance and I loved that.

My parents' politics were left and at some point they had been aligned with the CP though I have no idea to what depth. I know that after the revelations of Stalin's atrocities they were believers no more. But civil rights and other humanitarian causes were somehow conveyed to us, maybe by what they chose to listen to as far as music and news. They both belonged to unions and I knew from an early age not to cross a picket line. We signed on to WBAI shortly after it came on the air. They loved classical music and folk and I knew about the Weavers, Woody Guthrie and Pete Seeger along with Bach, Beethoven and Mozart.

There was no doubt that we were Jewish but what was it that made us so? For two summers I went to a YMCA camp in North Jersey. A friend had found it and the price was probably right. The first year I was 13. On Sundays they had chapel service outdoors on nice benches with a view of the surrounding hills. There was a huge, to me, cross on one side of the benches. I did not feel comfortable being there but not sure I could have told you why, had you asked. But I liked the setting and not to go would have made me conspicuous – not what a self-conscious 13 year old needs. I wrote to my parents and asked if I could be a Christian for the summer. How naive but sincere. My parents must have had a laugh at that but maybe also did some soul searching as to how they were raising me and my sister. No idea, because aside from a return letter telling me that it was okay to go to the services but that I did not have to become a Christian, it was never mentioned again as far as I recall.

Another instance was when I wanted a Christmas tree with presents under it, naturally. They went along with some of the Xmas stuff but when I said that I wanted to open the presents on Xmas morning and we were going away that morning, they said: "We have our traditions and they have theirs." I didn't challenge them but looking back now I see that their being Jewish was never in question though the practice of it was nearly non-existent.

I knew they were atheists or agnostic, as my mother once qualified, and that has passed on to me. But interestingly enough, when my mother was quite old, frail and far advanced in her dementia, she would say periodically, "I'm ready to meet my maker." She had definitely had enough. Not thinking I would get any kind of answer, I didn't ask her who she thought of as her maker. It might have been interesting.

So back to my cousin, Michael...He is my mother's sister's first son and was in the States to study sculpture at the Art Student's League in NYC. He and his wife, Rivka, lived near us on the Grand Concourse and often came to Friday night dinner. Our neighborhood was predominately Jewish but not many were orthodox. HH had not crossed my path. He had been in South Africa where his father was a shaliach for the Jewish Agency and while he visited them there he got a job at the moshava where, coincidentally, Ariel was the shaliach which is how Ariel Hurwitz (from GalOn) connected to my family. So he knew about HH and worked at Shomria. I was at home on those Friday nights and he asked me why I was so I said, "Where should I go?" I was in high school at Bronx Science and my friends there were from all over the city and beyond. We didn't meet on weekends. "Go to the movement," he said. Without too much explanation he told me how to get to Ken Hachoresh on Burnside Avenue and I went one winter Friday night when I was 15 ½.

And even though I was greeted in Polish because two Polish girls came in just before I did, I stayed and didn't look back. Seeing the happy chaos of boys and girls running madly around thrilled me. And their wearing jeans was a big plus. Soon I got the knack of the Hebrew words used to refer to what happened there and got to know the people and why they were there, I was hooked. I loved the idea of kibbutz though I was not convinced that all Jews should go to Israel. My parents were not Zionists despite where my grandparents and aunt were.

They were okay with me being in the movement but when I wanted to leave college and go to the chava, they were the most angry I had seen them.

Though I have little to do with being Jewish now, HH is not responsible for that. In fact, had I not been in HH I would probably not have gone to Israel to live. I was on track to go west before joining and would most likely have ended up where I am now. If not for friends I made on GalOn, who now live in a town near me, I would probably not celebrate holidays at all. I feel like an impostor or alien at services in synagogues the few times I have gone. Though, because of the Hebrew, I recognize parts of it and always enjoy the singing. Being in HH was an enriching experience and living in Israel for 11 years had a big part in making me who I am, for better or worse. I have often thought of returning but have reservations so that hasn't happened. Some of those years were a little wilder and crazier than was healthy but I would not trade them and the HH years for anything. Having this group of people I can connect to, some of whom I haven't seen for 50 years, is a testament to the value of those shared experiences.

Dancing at Ken HaChoresh between Teddy (Theo) Vermont and Yechiel (Marty) Felder

Lenor de Cruz, March 2021 - My Hashomer Experience

I was going to title this "A Guatemalan/Irish, Italian/German/Russian Christian Scientist finds her Jewish Identity" but it seemed a bit long.

Sometime during my freshman year of high school, I was asked by a friend if I would be interested in going into Los Angeles to a meeting of a Jewish youth group, a socialist-Zionist youth organization, called Hashomer Hatzair. This friend happened to be the son of one of my parents' close political friends. That first Friday evening at Hashomer I felt a sense of belonging I rarely felt in my high school.

In hindsight, of course, I could trace this feeling to my particular family history. The summer after third grade, my family moved from the high desert of Lancaster, California to an unincorporated, then rural, area of L.A. County (about 20 miles from Los Angeles) where my father was finally able to get a tenured teaching job. During the years before high school, I had already experienced my parents hosting rehearsals in our living room of a "Negro History Program" with music and readings, and a multi-racial, multi-ethnic cast of my parents' friends. The first demonstration I ever attended was a "Hands Off Cuba" rally in 1960 with a close family friend. I listened to my father's records, "Talking Union", Leadbelly, Josh White, Odetta, Harry Belafonte, and Burl Ives before ever hearing Elvis. I loved the Limelighters and the Weavers, though I do have a memory of slow dancing to "Teen Angel" at an eighth grade dance.

As I entered high school, I remember feeling quite alienated and trying to figure out how to fit in. The feeling was quite the opposite when I entered the ken on Melrose that Friday night. I immediately felt like I had found my place. I felt an affinity with the kids my age and older. I loved the folk dancing, and I have a memory of a group of several slightly older boys with guitars on the sidewalk just outside the door of the ken that has stayed with me to this day.

After several Friday nights with various parents driving us into the city and back, and for reasons I now can't remember, I wasn't able to continue going into the city that first year. But by my sophomore year, my friend, Avi was now driving himself and others into L.A. every week, so I had a ride I could count on. I enjoyed every moment. I felt more of a kinship with these Jewish kids from Fairfax than I ever did with my high school peers. As I said, I especially enjoyed folk dancing and participated in several performances. I also appreciated the study groups and discussions we had about Marx, Hegel, Herzl and sometimes sex. I felt comfortable with the way all of us were treated equally, boys and girls, younger and older. It felt so much saner to me than the high school cliques, where you worried about what you wore, how you looked and who you were friends with.

In the summer following my sophomore year in 1963, I attended Camp Shomria at Bellows Lodge, Big Bear Lake. I had never been to a summer camp and I enjoyed it immensely. During the years I was in Hashomer, I learned quite a lot about Jewish culture, traditions and history, like Purim, Pesach, Hanukkah, Lag B'Omer because there was usually an activity and educational discussion associated with each.

By this time, I had gotten my chultzah, had chosen my Hebrew name, Lilit, had learned to write it in Hebrew, and was singing the Israeli national anthem every Friday night. I was not only coming in on Fridays, but was spending the weekend with my new friends, going to Playa del Rey, listening to the newest Joan Baez album in someone's house, and always finding a ride home on Sunday with whomever else had spent the night from "the other valley". This was a whole new world for me

I later learned that one of the adult leaders of Hashomer from Israel had suggested that I shouldn't be a member because I wasn't Jewish. That recommendation was rejected by the shomrim, and it was only later that as I began talking to my mother about her ancestry, I discovered that her grandparents were Jewish (from either Germany or Russia/Prussia), her mother was Jewish, therefore she was Jewish, therefore I was Jewish. Interestingly, sometime in the 1930s both of my grandmothers had been drawn to the teachings of Mary Baker Eddy and Christian Science, so both my father and mother independent of each other, were raised by single mothers who were Christian Scientists. Nevertheless, while I was a member of Hashomer I embraced the ideals and goals and the history of the "Young Guard" and at the same time, stopped attending Christian Science Sunday School, also deciding I didn't believe in God. Both my parents were very happy that I was involved with Hashomer.

The summer after my junior year of high school, I joined five other shomrim in a "carry-all" driven by Baruch (from Israel), on a five-day trip from Los Angeles to Camp Shomria in Liberty, New York with a week-long stopover in Hightstown, New Jersey. We spent a week at the Hechalutz farm where I thoroughly enjoyed digging ditches, scrubbing the kitchen floor, bailing hay, and various other chores. There was something very appealing to me about 18-year olds living on and operating a farm for a year preparing for aliyah to Israel. I loved the idea of the kibbutz and wrote a paper in my English class about the kibbutz. Some of my classmates joked that I must be advocating "free love" since the kibbutz seemed to them like some kind of hippie commune. It didn't help that this was after I had returned from New York with a woven Greek shoulder bag from Greenwich Village and a peace button that I wore to school. This would not be news on the west side of L.A., but had never been seen at my high school in El Monte!

My participation in Hashomer finally came to a close after I received a letter from Donny asking me to step up and take on a leadership role with a younger group of shomrim. I knew I had to make a decision about whether to continue on this path, so I asked the wisest shomer I knew, Rafael Klorman, to explain Zionism to me. Finally, with a clearer understanding of Zionism, but with a solid commitment to socialist ideals, I decided to officially leave the movement. I felt I did not have inside me what it would take to guide and inform a younger group of shomrim about their culture and traditions since I had not grown up with those and they hadn't been internalized.

The friendships and values imparted by those formative years spent in Hashomer have stayed with me a lifetime.

In the photo below are: Elana, Dvora (Dorothy), Rachel (Rochelle), Chava (Evelyn), Lilit (Lenor) - LA Ken

Margie Ben Dov (Hechtman) Jerusalem

Hi, I read this last night in a book I'm reading and I thought it very applicable to the way we are all writing and trying to keep in contact. "People you knew when you were teenagers, the ones who saw your stupidest haircut and the most embarrassing things you've done in your life, and they still cared about you after all that: they're not replaceable, you know?" Tana French

I grew up in Brooklyn, one of four siblings, with a large extended family. My parents came to America when they were children, spoke Yiddish and instilled in us a feeling of pride that we're Jewish and almost disdain towards those who weren't. (Why almost?) As a child I pitied those children who didn't celebrate Chanukah and was sure that America joined the fighting in WWII to save the Jews. That's how important I felt we were (a child's perception). We had a kosher home and celebrated the holidays without the presence of god. Once a month we had a family circle meeting on my father's side. The amount of food and the decibels reached were impressive. Mah Jong, poker, pinochle and children running around screaming and everyone eating. The only time I remember when it got a bit hushed was when my father's two remaining cousins from Poland would speak to the adults about the war. I am named after an aunt on my mother's side who was killed in Auschwitz along with the rest of the family who never made it to America.

We would spend our summers, or parts of it, in the Catskills. My grandfather on my father's side tried farming there in the 1920s but left not being able to make a living. (https://www.jstor.org/stable/3742724?seq=1) My father's sister owned a hotel in Liberty on the other side from Shomria and those were the happiest days of my childhood. It wasn't elegant: army surplus beds and blankets that itched, one bathroom on each floor for all the guests. Most were relatives and I think that's why my aunt eventually had to close. They probably didn't pay. We picked the blueberries that were served for breakfast and my cousin would say," Gey essen" on the loudspeaker when dinner was being served. Wherever we turned, we, the children, were surrounded by people who loved us. That helped, to some degree, to get us through the hard times at home.

My reason for joining HH was not for any ideology whatsoever. I wanted to learn Hebrew so I could go to services (something my family never did except for my father's father}. Mimi Gloger, as she wrote, heard of a place where they taught Hebrew for free. We didn't know then that the price would be our very tender minds and us being uprooted from our families. Mimi and I have known each other since the age of 11 and before HH we spent many moments of hysterical laughter, unfortunately sometimes in school. The first meeting there was no Hebrew, only Marxism. But very soon I was sucked in by the dancing and the singing and the wonderful, talented and quirky kids who I felt so much, most of the time, a part of. My best memories are of Mosh Choref and of our socks drying in front of the fire. I could go on and on but all of you have put it so well, so I won't.

I did not go on aliyah with the garin. I waited a year and went straight to Jerusalem. A few months later I met my soon to be husband. I basically cut off ties with mostly everyone and felt perfectly at home with all of Shmulik's friends. Mimi has always been in my life, not on a daily basis, but she is there. Calling after each explosion in Jerusalem during the second intifada to make sure we are all ok and just reminding me there was a legitimate life before Israel. I am also very fortunate to have Mencher and Lewis here in Jerusalem. It means a lot to me.

My first year I studied in the Rubin Academy of Music and Dance with Meri and Tova but after a year, I moved to Tel Aviv and studied in a teachers' college.

After I got married, we moved to Kansas where my husband did his masters in music therapy. I worked in the Hebrew Academy in Kansas City. I won't go into how I lied to get in and screwed up the kashrut of the whole place without telling anyone.

Three years later we returned to Israel and only when I stepped on the plane, did I realize I didn't want to go back. Being here, the first years after we returned, were difficult especially when my girls were born. But here I am, 43 years later. The hardest part for me was, and is, not having my family nearby. B.C. (before corona) the four of us have even had trips together and we all traveled back and forth. Now we have a weekly zoom call.

 I taught art at a neighborhood elementary school. Teaching Israeli children is not for the weak of heart but when I look back, even though there were some difficult times and I never worked so hard in my life, I see it as an amazing and positive experience. To have a job where you can be creative and where you make a difference in so many lives, is a privilege. Even to this day, I will run into some of my children and they will give me a hug and a kiss, some in uniforms.

I have been very active, going to protests and signing endless petitions and voting for left-wing parties without much success. Recently I was feeling really despaired and totally helpless to change anything but then it hit me, I have succeeded by having three wonderful children (did you really think I wouldn't speak of my children not to mention my eight grandchildren?) who are free thinkers, liberal, pluralistic contributing members of society. I know of someone who said he finally figured out why he studied trigonometry...so he could teach his children.

Am I sorry I'm here? I'm not sorry that I'm not living in America. I hate the occupation and it has not given us one moment of joy or honor, only heartbreak on both sides. But could I live in a country where some of its citizens have been and still are suppressed and oppressed for centuries? We all just go on with our lives and hope to make a change wherever we can. I, for one, just want to concentrate my time now on family and friends. It just seems healthier than agonizing all the time.

Well, I've been ranting enough and this is from someone who wasn't sure if she wanted to contribute anything.

Stay well. Hope you are all vaccinated by now.

Margie

Upper left, Margie with others, on seminar
Left - Margie with Nechama
Above - Margie and Talya (Carol)

Meri Wallace – Meri Libuser, Sheepshead Bay, Long Island, PO Box 728, Amagansett, NY

One day, when I was ten, I was walking home from school and I suddenly felt somebody kick water into my boots. I turned around and saw two girls who were older and taller than me. Somehow, I knew they were Irish. They clearly were following me home. Suddenly they called out "Dirty Jew." I remember instantly feeling confused and upset. The words tore into me. I had no clue that I was experiencing antisemitism.

I started walking quickly and since we were only half a block from my house, I was soon in the entranceway of my building. The girls kept repeating horrible phrases to me and slowly but surely cornered me against a wall. I don't know where it came from but I exploded and I lunged at these two girls – punching and hitting them. I would have been overcome by them but luckily a neighbor came by and chased them away. I felt like they had put a knife through my heart. Being Jewish was something I loved and it was my identity even at that young age.

I grew up in a family that was far left of left. I was spoon-fed on Marxism, Lenin and Russia. My parents met in the Communist Party and they were all about standing up for the best values.

It wasn't easy growing up in the fifties in Coney Island as a red diaper baby. I felt all alone because my ideas were so different from my friends, and not acceptable. They were dangerous too, in an era of HUAC (*House Un-American Activities Committee*). I used to have a heart attack when I went to retrieve the mail and would find a copy of the *Daily Worker*.

We spent our summers in Golden's Bridge, a very lefty community in Westchester County. In this environment we were visited by Pete Seeger. We sang union songs, spirituals and folk songs. At the same time that we had this left liberal strand to our lives, my parents strongly cherished Jewish history and culture. In our summer community, we even had Israeli counselors who taught us Israeli folk dancing and songs.

My parents sent me to learn Yiddish at a Shula on Surf Avenue in Coney Island. My teacher had been in the Russian Revolution and lost an arm, which fascinated me no end and I couldn't stop staring at it. A powerful thing happened to me there in this little room... I fell in love with Israel. When we read in our history books about the pioneers turning the desert into green fields it evoked in me a passion and a love of the country. I decided I would go there.

So these two strands – the left me and the Jewish me led me to Hashomer.

One day I was in the cafeteria at Sheepshead Bay High School and I heard the strains of my favorite Israeli folk song: Erev Shel Shoshanim. I quickly walked over, eager to sing with whoever was singing. It was that day that I met Mimi, then Gloger, and Ira, still Orenstein, and they invited me to come to Ken Masada on Church and Flatbush Avenues.

I fit into Hashomer Hatzair like a glove. The beauty of it for me was that I found a new year-round community where I could be myself. Everybody was progressive and we all loved Israel. How wonderful!!!

I participated in the 1965 seminar on Kibbutz Mishmar Haemek. I roomed with Ira and Laurie, and we were the lucky survivors of the great fire of '65. The kibbutznikim probably still talk about it.

I returned and Tzvi Brazil and I ran Ken Mishmar Hanamal for a few years. We left to go to the chava after the Six Day War, married in 1967 at the age of 20, and left for Kibbutz Galon. After a year, we moved to Jerusalem, and I attended the Rubin Academy of Music and Dance with Margie and Tova, and Tzvi went to The Bezalel Art Academy.

We had a son, Michael in 1973. Yes! It was in the middle of the Yom Kippur War. When the war broke out, I was nine months pregnant, and Tzvi left to the front within an hour. He ended up in Egypt. Thank god for Mimi and Zoie, who had become our dear friends when we moved to Jerusalem, and supported me through that rough time. And thank god for Pnina Isseroff who stayed with me and made the call to Zoie who drove me to Hadassah to deliver our son. Yechiel was great too. He was driving for Magen David Adom and delivered milk to me in the middle of a snow storm!

We had many close friends in Jerusalem including Tzippy and Murray Kleiner and Shoshana and Shimon Kochavi. We all shared the beginnings of our children's lives together.

Tzvi and I returned to the states in August, 1975. We divorced shortly after that and I taught dance for many years. Later, I remarried and became a social worker, specializing in child and family therapy and child development. I began writing parenting books, "Keys to Parenting Your Four Year Old, " and "Birth Order Blues". I wrote a column for Sesame Parents Magazine and had fun as a parenting expert on TV.

A little later I became a playwright and had years of writing and producing my work. My biggest theater achievement has been, "Tango Fever" produced off-Broadway. I currently live in Amagansett, LI a great escape during Covid, and am writing a new book called, "The Secret World of Children."

What can I say about Hashomer? It was a great period of my life and opened up a whole world to me. I still do Israeli folk dancing with many chevra from the movement, from all over the world. I even danced with Marty Braff in Manhattan and we danced well together. The thing that I am most grateful for is the movement gave me all of you. And I am so pleased that you are all still in my life. Chazak V'amatz!

JUN • 65

Michael Alexander and Hashomer Hatzair

I joined Hashomer Hatzair shortly after starting junior high school. A friend from elementary school, who ended up not going to my junior high, invited me to join him for an evening of films and folk dancing because he had gotten a notice about this special event at his school. We went together and the folk dancing hooked me. I had done a lot at my secular Jewish Sunday school so the transition to the new dances was easy and fun for me. My friend did not become a regular but I started going weekly for the activities.

I was a distinct minority at my junior high school. We lived rather close to Pico and Crenshaw for those familiar with Los Angeles. I went to the junior high that served the heavily Black community just to the south of us. The majority of my elementary school classmates transferred to a less integrated junior high. My school was about 70% Black, 10% Japanese-American (many of whom had no idea that their parents and older relatives had been interred by the US during WWII), 10% white and 10% English-as-a-Second-Language students. There were very few Jews so HH gave me a connection to my heritage and family values.

My first madrich was Chaim, my second was Donny Metzl, and my third was Yoel Krakowsky. I remember getting my chultza (blue shirt) and, eventually, my aniva (scarf).

One of my strongest early memories was planning for my first Lag BaOmer tiyul. My grandmother lived with us at that time and she knew that I loved her chopped liver sandwiches. She made me two for lunch for that day. It was only in the minutes before lunch that I was informed that we were all going to create a lunch "koopa" (tossing everything onto the table for everyone to share). I had been dreaming of those two sandwiches not just all day, but also the days leading up to the tiyul knowing what my grandmother was going to make for me. I was not happy about this idea and balked at the notion of losing one or both of my chopped liver sandwiches. In spite of being a fussy eater, I was okay with tossing in the rest of the lunch and somehow I ended up getting at least one of my sandwiches (I may have gotten both).

The other standout memory of that tiyul was hearing that there was a girl who had climbed very high into one of the trees near our lunch area. I loved tree climbing and joined her and the others. The girl was Elana Rappaport who had recently joined HH and we became close friends for years.

Among my other memories is going to my first summer moshava which was held in Arroyo Grande in San Luis Obispo County. HH rented a church camp that had a large rotunda where we met for all large group activities. It really impressed me (I was 13 by then). I also remember the food. Not that good and the bread was either white or brown (wheat?) Weber's Bread. We never had bread of that sort at our house so this was real culture shock for me.

Sometime after attending HH meetings for a number of months, my father shared with me that he had been a member of HH as a teenager in Berlin. I don't know why he kept it as a secret that long but I was proud to hear that he had been involved a generation earlier. Knowing that association of his led to an interesting professional/personal encounter more than a decade later. More on that at the end of this narrative.

I was a member of HH for five years. My parents got involved with Americans for a Progressive Israel. Somehow, my mother and one of her best friends became the cooks at moshava (and got their younger sons involved – my brother Srul and his best friend Shachar) where they cooked for years. I remember discovering Barton Flats through the many camps that HH rented there. I loved the hikes up to Dollar Lake and the regular swimming trips to Jenks Lake.

I was about as regular as anybody for those five years. My father, a construction electrician, got involved in wiring the new moadon on Melrose near La Brea. I remember discovering Pinks before it became the tourist attraction that it is today. Our favorite cook was an old fellow named Boris. When Baskin Robbins opened practically next door to the moadon, I remember patronizing regularly to see if they had any broken cones they'd give away for free!!

I also remember being introduced to Hebrew. My secular Jewish Sunday school had focused on Yiddish which was frowned upon at HH. I remember working with others to create a choreography for one of our folk dances for some kind of mass Zionist group event at Griffith Park's Greek Theater; trying to learn Hebrew; getting introduced to HH's approach to socialism and Zionism; and learning about other values-based concepts. We certainly aligned with progressive causes in the US but a stand-out memory is how we behaved during the national grieving after the assassination of President Kennedy.

Our shaliahs at the time were Ariyeh and Ada Levitt. We had already scheduled activities for the Saturday of the funeral which Ariyeh would not cancel. Even Democrats were not progressive enough for HH. So I was at the moadon when the rest of the country was glued to their TVs. I guess I could find the entire funeral coverage on YouTube today but, for years, I felt I missed an important national event that day.

As I was about to enter 12th grade, I realized that I had to think about what HH expected of me – going on seminar and eventually moving to Israel. I was not motivated to make that move as I had other career goals (totally unrealized) in the performing arts. I wanted to study mime with Marcel Marceau. Some time during my last year of high school, I left HH but continued to be peripherally involved due to my parents' API involvement and my mother's continued work as a cook at Moshava. My brother ultimately did make aliyah and has lived on Kibbutz Shomrat since the early 70s. Today, his youngest son and family live there as well while his older son and daughter live elsewhere in the country.

Now for the interesting connection story referenced above. Some time in my mid-twenties, when I was the General Manager of the Aman Folk Ensemble, a local ethnic dance and music company that ultimately toured the world and created a significant national reputation in the arts community, one of the local synagogues engaged the company to perform. During a meeting with the Rabbi's wife to talk about the event, she asked how I got started in folk dancing. I was reluctant to mention HH because of its anti-religious views but felt compelled to tell her about my love of folk dancing at HH meetings. Once I said that, she told me that she had been a member of HH and it turned out she had been a member in Berlin. I connected her to my father who she had not seen since the 30s. The two of them reconnected and shared lots of information. My father got contact information for other ex-shomrim living in Israel who he and my mother visited during their trips to see my brother and family.

I don't see many of the others from my HH days very often. Some of you may remember that the only other Zionist organization that we would associate with was Habonim. I remember meeting former County Supervisor/City Councilman Zev Yaroslavsky when our two organizations attended each others' events and he, ultimately, married one of our fellow Shomrim, Yael Edelstein, who, unfortunately, passed away a few years ago. We crossed paths intermittently through the years.

Hashomer Hatzair was extremely important to me during my five years of membership. I am very glad that I was involved. Thank you for the opportunity to write this missive. It brought back many memories. I also realized how much of popular culture I missed/avoided due to the intense commitment we all made to HH.

Mimi Tanaman, aka Mimi Gloger

Formerly of Ken Masada, co-founder of Ken Mishmar Hanamal, Brooklyn Today: Copywriter/translator/author, Community theatre actor/director
Aliya: March 1966. Currently resident of Raanana, Israel.
Education: BA, MA, Psychology, Hebrew University of Jerusalem
Married +2; together with husband, Baruch, we have 5 children and 13 grandchildren.

Reflections on my Jewish upbringing, and the influence of Hashomer Hatzair

As a child, my Judaism was Passover and Hanuka, holidays celebrated with family, knowing that almost all my friends celebrated as we did, with everyone going to synagogue for Rosh Hashana and Yom Kippur. Matzot during Passover, latkes for Hanuka, and fasting at Yom Kippur – that was about the extent of it.
My sister and I briefly attended a Jewish Community Center Sunday school, where we learned Bible stories, drew pictures of Israel, with sand, palm trees and baskets of fruit, and dressed up for Purim.
The Keren Kayemet box for planting trees in Israel, was always a feature of our and our grandparents' homes.
Our "eggman" had numbers tattooed on his arm. I absorbed vague bits of information, understanding that this was related to terrible times for Jews in Europe.

A turning point was a magazine distributed in my junior high, with a heading on the cover "Making the Desert Bloom" and a picture of Israeli pioneers working in a field – work boots, short shorts, kova temble and all, and a small insert photo of PM Ben Gurion, looking like a kindly grandfather. My imagination took off. I wanted to be those people in the picture, to be part of the stream of history of my people, to become a pioneer in Israel.

As a toddler, I understood my grandfather with no problem. As I got older, I became aware that he was speaking a different language that I did not understand. I told my father, I'd like to learn his language. My father had been a member of Hashomer Hatzair in his youth, and was still friends with a man who remained involved and was part of the parent organization, API. Not differentiating between Yiddish and Hebrew (they're both Jewish languages, aren't they?) he contacted his friend for details of the nearest ken, and off I went to Ken Masada to the Hebrew Chug. One day, I joined the Ideology Chug run by Tzvi Body, which met right after the Hebrew one. I was intrigued both by the ideology and by Tzvi. I dropped Hebrew and carried on with my new learning, including reading Marx's "Dialectical Materialism". The ken, the ideas, the camaraderie, all drew me in. And here was a Jewish identity beyond our foreign-sounding grandparents. It was a Jewish identity that was young and proud and optimistic, and fit right in with ideas of pioneering in Israel. I was sold.

Hashomer Hatzair had libraries of books I hadn't encountered before. One summer at Camp Shomria, I walked off every day into the woods to be alone with my book – The Massacre of European Jewry. I cried my way through the book that summer. That was my encounter with the Holocaust.

Summers at Shomria, and winter at Mosh Choref, were times of growth and learning. I loved the lectures with Natan Yonatan, learning Israeli songs with his wife Tzfira, creating dance performances (with Mimi W.), and it was at Shomria that I had my first experience directing a show, something I've done quite a lot of in later life with a community theatre. I also learned that with a stern look and two fingers in the air, even a short quiet girl can get a hundred kids to be quiet. Some other favorite memories involve performing Israeli songs and dances in New York synagogues, while Margie and I did our best not to look at each other in our attempt to control the giggles threatening to explode. And among the 'chevre' of Hashomer, it was a place of music, echoing my other summer camp folk music experiences, which I loved.

Seminar, six months on Kibbutz Dalya, and an opportunity to explore the country, was another wonderful experience and only served to strengthen my resolve that Israel was where I wanted to live.

My aliyah came early, just one year later, as I was faced with a choice. My boyfriend and his family were leaving for Israel. Back in the 60s, the only acceptable options were either to wave goodbye forever, or get married. Off he went with his family, while I arranged the wedding. Five months later he returned to make me his bride. A week after the wedding we returned to Israel, two married teenagers.

We lived in Jerusalem and attended the Hebrew University. Little by little, more of our friends from Hashomer arrived in Israel, and we became a community. I had always planned to join a kibbutz, but after another six months on Kibbutz Barkai, on summer break and during the Six Day War, I felt that kibbutz life was too limiting and insular. Meanwhile, many of our friends who made aliya to a kibbutz, began joining us in Jerusalem instead.

During our first year in Jerusalem, Zoie and I met a British couple who played banjo, fiddle, guitar and dulcimer, and invited us to perform with them. I soon learned to play the double bass, while Zoie became proficient on the mandolin and autoharp, and we spent the next ten years or so performing around the country, bluegrass in Hebrew, with radio and TV appearances and even on the stage in Caesarea. That was great fun. I became the main emcee of our group, telling jokes and stories. After the group broke up (and some years later our marriage, parting me from my double bass), I joined a community theatre and continued spending time on stage. I remember my mother also appearing in NY in community theatre productions, and I was always in school and summer camp productions.

So having decided psychology would be a more stable profession than acting, being on stage has been the single most consistent thread throughout my life... that and writing.

I established my own copyrighting company, hi-Text, in 1998, and am still at it. I have also published a book, translated a couple of children's books in rhyme (all available on Amazon) and am about to publish my novel about the Ethiopian journey to Israel and their continued journey for acceptance. I am the pro bono copywriter for ESRA (www.esra.org.il), Israel's largest English speaking non-profit, dedicated to helping olim acclimate and volunteering through their many education and welfare projects helping weaker sectors of society. Baruch, my British Israeli husband, was national chairman of ESRA for several years, which led to my involvement in the organization and to my joining one of their trips to Ethiopia, accompanying teenagers on a Roots Journey. It was after that trip that I felt ready to embark on my novel.

I have never regretted my decision to live in Israel, and I am grateful to Hashomer Hatzair for having played a part in getting me here. Living in Israel, you are expressing your Judaism just by being here. Your children grow up learning their people's history, from Biblical times on, and we celebrate more of the holidays in Israel, even without attending synagogue, than we ever would have if I'd stayed in the States.

Friendships made during your teen years, when formative experiences are shared, are friendships that last a lifetime. Nonetheless, it is quite remarkable that such a large group of people have maintained contact and friendships for more than 50 years! I am proud to have been a member of this dynamic organization that dared to fight the Nazis in Warsaw.

Here's to Hashomer Hatzair, to shared experiences, and to Shomrim everywhere! Chazak Ve'amatz!

Mimi, Yehuda and Batsheva

Mimi (Wasserman) Wolf – Montana – Queens, NY

January 31, 2021

My earliest awareness of Jewish identity came from my father. He was born in Toronto, Canada and found his way to settle on Kibbutz Kfar Bloom before Israel was a state. That period of time was the happiest of his life. He always regretted leaving kibbutz and a girlfriend whose photograph he retained. Peretz served in the Merchant Marines aboard ships in the Mediterranean. His ship was torpedoed and he floated about until he was picked up and deposited in Alexandria, Egypt. From there he made his way back to North America being held on Ellis Island for one month, for a reason unknown to me.

When my father spoke of the Holocaust, which had clearly traumatized him, it terrified me. I was frightened by my Jewish identity. He also expressed great pride relating to Israel. As I had no siblings and my mother was ill most of my life, Jewish holidays were acknowledged but not particularly joyful events. There was no conveyance of religiosity though Dad had a tallit and his mother's Tanach, both of which I still have. At night he would read me the tales of Chelm which amused us both. My parents spoke Yiddish when they didn't want me to understand. I remember them hosting a Farband meeting in our apartment one night. For the most part, like my mother's mental illness, Judaism was one more dark burden.

When I found the Tnuah the things my father had shared began to make sense. I then had a Jewish framework to attach to and build upon. My madrichim, Hillel Schenker and Tzippy Kleiner, imbued me with both pride in Israel and the social values I retain to this day. My kvutzah and shichva became my family. Holidays became joyful and meaningful, music and dancing were expressions of Jewish joy. Eydie, Dottee, Shuli, Ariela were my sisters. It was just such a relief not to be lonely and sad anymore.

Our Seminar in the fall of 1964 was the seminal moment in forming my Jewish identity. I had been released from the prison of my unhappy childhood into a life of learning and adventure. I loved the rural setting of Kibbutz Dalia. Ultimately, I defaulted on aliyah only because I wanted to study dance and could see that path forward in the US. Natan Yonatan offered me a studio on Galon but I was only prepared to study, not teach. So one decision led to another and another and then to Montana.

I have no God gene and cannot relate to religiosity other than culturally. I see both the dark and the light in humanity, the ugliness and the beauty religion inspires. Humans are tribal by nature. I belong to the Jewish tribe. Ours is a learned and industrious one and since 1947 it is one of protective strength.

In Israel, not Montana, I feel most at home. Like my father, I never managed that permanent physical transition. But Israel is surely where my heart resides. Amongst my best friends I count those I have retained from the years we shared in HH.

Mimi W.

Bonnie, Mimi and Nechama

Miriam Beinin - How family, Hashomer Hatzair and politics shaped me

I grew up in a 'Jewish' resort town on the shores of Lake Michigan during the 1950s and 1960s. Despite the large influx of Jews to the lakeside hotels in the summers, there were very few Jewish families who lived year-around in our small town. Nonetheless, my mother, who was not religious but who had a spiritual connection to her Judaism, provided my sister and me with a strong sense of our Jewish heritage especially around the major holidays. My father, however, was an ardent atheist.

The only synagogue in South Haven was a conservative one and my sister and I attended both Hebrew and Sunday school until we were about 12. My sister chose to have a Bat Mitzvah, however, I chose to go to Camp Shomria instead – since my parents could not afford to fund both activities. My mother taught Sunday school at the synagogue so she could keep track of what we were learning. My father would not set foot inside any religious institution, although he did stand in the doorway of the synagogue during my sister's Bat Mitzvah – only to disappear the minute she finished chanting.

The holocaust was not a central theme that influenced my identity. We did not lose family in this way. My father however came from Ukraine with his family when he was ten and his traumatic memories of the pogroms he'd witnessed were something that left him emotionally fragile. Growing up, I rarely experienced antisemitism although my parents did experience anti-communist threats in the 1950s because they were pro-union. They were activists involved with various union organizing efforts as well as civil rights. They taught in literacy programs and were advocates for integration. These were controversial, left-wing positions to take in small-town America in the 1950s and they often made our family unpopular.

My parents owned a ten acre chicken farm and considered themselves socialists and because of this they wanted us to have a more progressive experience than the synagogue could provide – especially since this was during the McCarthy period.

Although my parents were not Zionists, the only progressive option they could find for furthering their daughters' education was Camp Shomria. So, in 1954 at the age of nine, I was sent to moshava – which I subsequently attended every year until I went away to college. At some point, the summer camp moved its operations from Michigan to Perth, Ontario.

In 1965, I took a break from college to participate in the seminar l'madrachim on Gal-on and Mishmar Haemek. There I met Joey Beinin who was 16 (I was 19). After returning from seminar, I resumed my college education and in the late 1960s became the rosh ken in Detroit.

Joey and I lived on the chava in Hightstown, NJ in 1969 and were in the garin that made the decision to close it. After marrying in 1970, we went on aliyah to Kibbutz Lahav with Joey's garin of 40. After about nine months, we realized we could not find our place there and decided to move to Jerusalem. We concluded that the kibbutz had not made adequate preparations for accepting us as potential members and instead treated us as they did their volunteers – young bodies available to do the work they no longer wanted to do. They housed us in unheated tzrifim along with the volunteers. The shared bet-shimush seemed a far walk from our poorly furnished one-room accommodations.

Prior to our arrival on the kibbutz, we had been involved in the Civil Rights movement. But at Lahav we found that the Arabs working alongside us as hired laborers were working on the lands from which they had been expelled. Joey learned these things while practicing his Arabic with the workers. This left us feeling guilty and extremely troubled. Concretely, we found it disturbing that the kibbutzniks refused to sit with these workers during lunch in the cheder-ochel. There were other ideological issues our shilchim had taught us that were no longer being upheld in the kibbutz and these things culminated in our feeling a certain betrayal. The romance of the kibbutz quickly faded as the day-to-day routines and the unsatisfying work assignments became the reality. The kibbutz had gone through a process from the time of its founding and had since moved on. We had not been part of that process and were stuck in the romance of a mythical past that we had been taught to believe.

The kibbutz sent those of us with minimal Hebrew to an ulpan in Be'er Sheva comprised primarily of Russian immigrants - most of whom were not Jewish. A kibbutznik would take us as far as the main road and leave us there to wait for the bus. Sometimes we would cross the road and take the bus going in the opposite direction spending the day in search of palatable glidah (ice cream) in Tel Aviv.

My disillusionment was also fueled by the job I was assigned which consisted of ironing four to five hours a day; a job I had done for years while growing up on the farm in Michigan, but now did not jive with my awakening feminist sensibilities. At first, we tried to hang on to the ideology we had been taught in HH, but it was not somehow compatible with the Israel in which we found ourselves in 1971.

After leaving Lahav, we lived in Jerusalem (Kiryat Yovel and later Katamon) for three years. In trying to adapt to the new reality we found ourselves in, we became part of the Israeli new left and began to meet Palestinians, many of whom became life-long friends. We participated in demonstrations with the Israeli Black Panthers and Siach and were lovingly mentored by the Kaminer family. Joey attended the Hebrew University while I worked in a school for autistic children in the hills above Jerusalem.

We had fled to Kibbutz Lahav on the heels of Joey's Vietnam draft status however, after three years in Israel, the Israeli army decided to claim him, so we eventually decamped to Boston and then to Ann Arbor to attend graduate school.

Just after our return from Israel in 1973, Joey's entire family decided to make aliyah. His parents are now deceased, but we try to visit his sister and brother – and the Kaminer family – annually.

In 1983, we left Ann Arbor and moved to Palo Alto/Stanford for Joey's job teaching history. I got a job as a transplant social worker at Stanford hospital and for the next 35 years we did not have a formal connection to Jewish institutions. We did belong to Jewish Voice for Peace based in Berkeley for many years beginning in the early 2000s, however, we're no longer active members. Being married to Joey, an outspoken advocate for Palestinian equal rights, also brought its challenges. At the time, those ideas were more controversial in certain circles than perhaps they are now.

Over the years we have traveled extensively and, besides Jerusalem, have lived for periods in Cairo, Oxford, and Paris.

Once our son was born in 1978, we began to celebrate the Jewish holidays at home more seriously. Jamie had a secular Bar Mitzvah when he turned 13 both in NY and Israel to accommodate both sides of the family. He attended a secular Sunday school in Palo Alto from age 7-13. When he was 17, he decided he wanted a "real" Bar Mitzvah and asked the rabbi of the conservative synagogue in Palo Alto if he could become a member (Joey and I did not join) so he could study for this. He chanted the entire service one Saturday in May, a date Joey picked for one of the lines from Parashat Achrei Mot Kedoshim: "do not stand idly by." Jamie continues to feel extremely connected to Judaism. In college he minored in Hebrew and Jewish Studies but does not belong to a temple. He is raising his daughter, age ten, to love her Jewishness and she is being sent to a reform synagogue in Portland at her mother's behest to begin her Bat Mitzvah lessons. During COVID Joey has zoom-taught her to read and speak Hebrew. We hope to take her to Israel when we can all safely travel again.

After Joey retired in 2019, we moved to Portland, OR to be closer to our son and granddaughter and joined Havurah Shalom, a progressive reconstructionist synagogue. Joey is more active than I – teaching classes on Middle East topics and is part of the Sanctuary and Tikkun Olam committees. He also co-chairs the education committee. I am still looking for my place.

I am Jewish – and an atheist. We celebrate holidays and Shabbat with our family in Portland. Every Shabbat Joey makes challah, we light candles and say the brachot.

We have continued this ritual even during COVID (maintaining precautions) with our son and granddaughter. These traditions have helped cement our family connections. In addition, our Israeli niece (Joey's brother's daughter) lives near us in Portland.

I do not regret my experiences in Hashomer or in Israel and although I no longer consider myself a Zionist as I did when I was young, Hashomer was important in informing and shaping me. When I'm in Israel, despite any criticisms, it often feels like "home".

My hope for Israel is embodied in the Jewish/Arab co-educational schools "Hand in Hand" (founded by Lee Gordon a member of our synagogue in Portland). I believe this exemplary model of co-existence to be the way forward toward an equitable and secure future for all.

Miriam Beinin
February 2021
Portland, OR

Philip Clement

I'm first generation Canadian from a large, secular, traditional, religious, opinionated, working class, very Jewish family. My Yiddish/Russian/Polish speaking parents were part of the huge European emigration of the '20s which resulted in Montreal becoming the heartbeat of Canadian Jewry, and the birthplace of the Bagel. eh. :-)

The influence of the tnua in my life started well before my birth. I'm fourteenth of fifteen grandchildren belonging to my beloved pious Russian/Chasidic grandparents (1870-1968). Twenty-five years before I was born the first grandchild, Issie, emigrated from Kiev as a pre-teen with my orthodox aunt and uncle. At seventeen he 'rebelled' and announced he's no longer going to wear a yarmulka. The years following are unknown to me, but this independent thinker one day found his way to Ken Gilboa and eventually joined the N. American garin headed for Ein Dor. As fate would have it his aliya was interrupted by WWII, after which he settled in Montreal and became a central pillar for the tnua and an articulate advocate for socialism, Zionism, and kibbutz. Issie was Danny Nachshen's father, our families dear and close. Issie founded the Canadian branch of Mapam (FPI) and was the 'Canadian equivalent' of Avraham Schenker, his colleague and friend.

It was through Issie's encouragement that my sister Nechama started going to the Montreal ken in the 50s often dragging her twin kid brothers with. She went on Machon in '57, shlichut to LA in '58, the chava in '59 and aliya with the Hazorea Garin in 1960 — a few months before my bar mitzvah. The next time my brother and I saw her was as 18 1/2 year olds on the porch of our tzrif on Dalia. The reunion was ecstatic, out of body like. Today my sister, in her 80s, is one of the beloved elders of Kibbutz Haogen, her three kids and eight grandchildren within a stone's throw.

And so, looking back, it seems natural that Danny, Peter, Philip, and my buddy across the street Warren Hill were some of the very first kovshim of the opening of Camp Shomria on gorgeous Lake Otty, in 1956. (!) Our madrichim were unsentimental, loving, practical and pragmatic. They granted us so much trust. We went on twelve mile overnights, learned scouting knots, to make a one match fire without paper, lash a lean-to, sharpen an ax, dig an outdoor fridge and where to look for falling stars and the Northern Lights. To keep thirst at bay on long hikes keep a small round pebble in your mouth. Back at Mosh we built a platform without nails high in the trees and stood on shmira looking out for the beer smelling nearby town troublemakers, the Perth Bums. We danced international folk dances and sang in every language. We studied lofty lefty Jewish idealism and shared our sweets stash in 'kupa'. We lived the 'hands-on, up-close and personal, outdoor, un-overprotected, pre-digital reality', embedded in nature, relationships activism and idealism. Without parents!

We were challenged and mentored in idealistic if not always enlightened ways. When Popeye heard a kid swearing he would wash his mouth out with a dry bar of soap. Pieces would stick in our teeth made us puke was disgusting. In response we formed a kids' vigilante protest lobby, went to battle our case and won. Over a madrich! Mosh! We never missed our parents. We dared our first kiss, learned to swim, had room to grow.

At around 15, having been at Mosh already seven times, I remember conceptualizing that my (12 month) year actually consisted of mostly Mosh, by far, with occasional annoying interruptions in the city, having to put up with adults, and go to dumb school. Finally we got back to the real world at Mosh.

I threw myself whole-heartedly into the tnua, lox, stock and aniva, and reciprocally the tnua took whatever it could from me. Any organization run on volunteer labour thrives on fanatic loyalty. My identity was the tnua. It was mutual, symbiotic, creative rich and vibrant. I was a madrich for many years, Rosh Ken, Rosh Mosh, Shaliach to Boston, and an activist in the Zionist community. My horizons expanded exponentially. I belong to only a handful of Canadians who saw Nechama star in "My Name Is Chana Szenesh", listened to Yehuda Bauer in the refet, helped collate *The Young Guard* in the lishka with Ami Sperber, and spent a day in the Borscht Belt around Liberty dancing and making a ruckus at resorts (I can't remember why.)

Yet there was another thread woven into my commitment which I think deserves a nod. From a very young age I was ashamed of my sensitive nature, and ashamed that I was ashamed. I internalized a brutal self doubt and lived expecting humiliation at any moment. If I could only figure out the rules. At times when my inner world did slip out "oh you're too sensitive" was the familiar refrain from peer and adult alike. I had no skills to negotiate boundaries, let alone understand what was really going on, so of course I did what any self-respecting, overly-sensitive, highly-empathic, self-doubting, second-born identical twin would do... I got depressed! :-)

Alas, as fate would have it, depression wasn't my last station. I also created a self-assured, socially-adept, outgoing wanna-be suave persona, modeled of course on the comes-by-it-naturally chutzpa, charisma, positivity & panache of my dear ex-womb mate. As strategies to avoid humiliation go, all this was well below my awareness. But lo and behold it was the social, spiritual, and cultural quintessence of Camp Shomria, and in my later teens the tnua, where I could drop my over thinking and simply let my enthusiasm for life flow. Yes, I was a proud secular Jew, Zionist, socialist, and kibbutz advocate, but the idealistic and positive undertones of the tnua, and the obviousness (to me) of how to succeed in such a hermetic body politic meant I could figure out what was going on. Given my hidden fragility, if there had been a less inviting atmosphere, I don't know if my politics and principles would have kept me on that path. It was much more nuanced than black and white, but my first allegiance was to a safe social milieu.

My intended life trajectory – to fulfill myself as a secular Jew on kibbutz – was genuine and sincere but not necessarily from my depths. Went on aliya to Gal On only to quickly feel lost and unbearably lonely. The tnua was gone, my social life was gone, I had no place to hide from inner demons, and was ill-prepared for the transition from Mr. Canadian Tnua to "echad mi ha Amerikaiyim". The garin was also going through their individual integration tzouris and the days looked bleak. Chaotic months later, before the mass exodus from Galon, I took my kibbutz girlfriend for a visit to Lahav, designated for the coming garin. "Welcome to your new home." I said, as we stepped off the bus. "Ma pitom!?! There is no way I am moving here!" We got married on Lahav and lived there almost five more years. The young idealistic 'sabra' flavour resonated with my image of kibbutz and I felt my idealism and optimism return. My work ethic served me well and opened many doors and hearts on the kibbutz. I started working in agriculture, could spend 8 - 10 hours mostly alone on a tractor then immerse myself in the social intensity of the dining room, moadon and communal living. My Israeli and Bedouin instructors became dear friends and taught me generously and with wisdom: "It's easy to drive a tractor – it's hard to take care of it." I was given more and more responsibility and bigger and bigger machinery to operate! I was a kibbutz photographer, in charge of the volunteers, in the kibbutz choir, chaperoned school trips and sat on the kibbutz secretariat. Lahav became my home and I was proud and protective of her.

Gradually though, I could feel a need to know myself better from the inside. Chugging down an entire bottle of Shabbat Red Wine and the consequent all night bowl hugging session was a bad beginning but with merit, and that never happened again. At kibbutz parties I would watch the volunteers erotically and exotically dance with utter abandon and knew I had to figure out how to be that free.

I was on a visit to Bet Zera when Jordanian fighter jets flew overhead. Sitting in a bomb shelter with the loud speaker giving unintelligible updates, I said to myself - Hey just a minute! Do those pilots know I'm Canadian AND a pacifist!?! It was an awakening moment and I made the choice to became an Israeli citizen which included being drafted. Thirteen months in the Israeli infantry was a crash course in confronting my demons, my limits, and my potential. I was twenty four and my sergeants were twenty. I did my best and had my moments, but emotionally was in over my head. In desperation I applied for an early discharge and literally jumped for joy when it came through. After five years away I boarded a plane back to Montreal, and to the beginning of my journey inwards.

I became a seeker. I went on vision quests with shamans, meditation intensives, and then in the most serendipitous circumstances discovered an Improvisational Dance Training. I became a Dance and Bodywork practitioner and used my empathic skills alongside the experience of planning a thousand pe'ulot to become a requested group instructor for several German Therapy institutes. Dance Improv and therapeutic touch were my go-to obsessions. I was not in any formal way a 'tradition practicing' Jew any longer, but I found the expression of my Jewishness in my heart, corny as it sounds. My uncles' teachings, both the orthodox ones and the secular, named kindness, generosity, love and service, respect for our parents and elders as cornerstones of Judaism. And so it be.

I visited Israel often traveling wide and staying at both Galon and Lahav. I so love the smells, the geography, the language, the food, the weather, and friends and family. There are large pieces of my heart in both kibbutzim, especially the fields. But Canada seduced me and held me. Then I married a shiksa from Germany and ended up living in her Heimat for ten years. :-)

Gabriele is my sun and moon, earth and sky. On our 38th anniversary I said to her: "We've been arguing about the same things for 38 years – when am I going to learn?" She clipped: "Stay with me for another 38 years and maybe you will." I adore her. She taught me that Xmas, Pesach, Rosh Hashanah and Easter all embrace the same essence: ritual celebration, family, friends, love, special food and presents. The rest is detail.

And I am delighted – as one of the token Canadians – :-) to be taking part in this precious collection of souls and wide casting of the 'net'.

Chazak!

Philip Clement
Interruption Farm
Qualicum Beach, Canada

Every time I think of my homeland
I think of yellow sand
I also think of big trees
that look so beautiful dressed
in green leaves.

And as the sun does set
I lay down and try to rest
But my head is full of thoughts
About the wars my ancestors fought.
And as I look a the Sea
I say Oh Israel
May the Lord Preserve Thee.

Danny Nachshen Grade V October 1957.

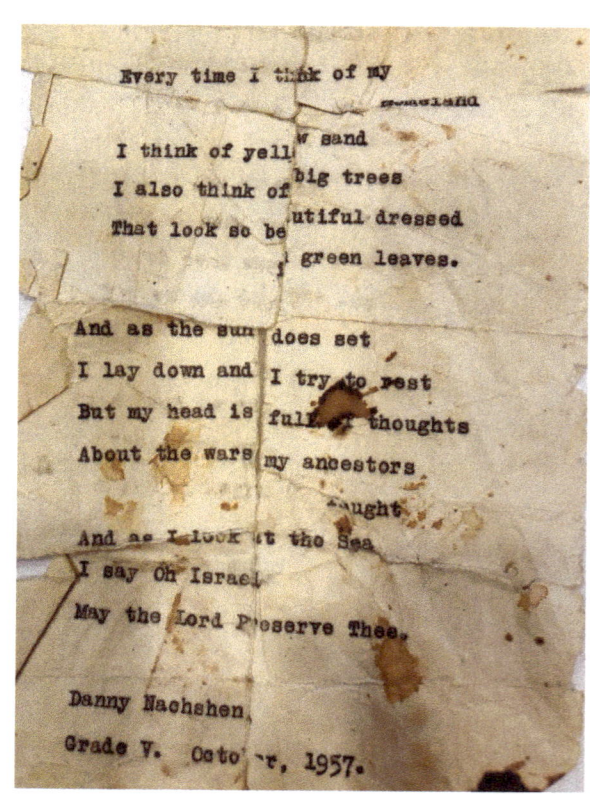

Nechama and her kid brothers saying good bye at Lod airport. Jan 1965.

Shellie Sherman/ Levy, Los Angeles, now Pittsburgh, retired from administrative positions and now enjoys painting in acrylic, collage, botanical art, and children's book illustration.

I didn't choose Hashomer. It chose me. My mother, Rivka Rosenberg, a Los Angeles native, met my father, Seymour Levy at the "Hashomer Bayit" in the early 1940s. He had driven a carload of shomerniks from his native Brooklyn to Los Angeles in his 1939 Pontiac. My parents married in 1943 and had three daughters. They had a strong belief in Zionism all their lives. Their sense of being Jews was tied to Zionism and the State of Israel and not to the Jewish religion or synagogues. My older sister, Chaviva, joined Hashomer when she was ten and left our family for her newly found Hashomer family. I followed her into the movement at age twelve. We spent years at the ken on Melrose Avenue listening to sichot and dancing Israeli dances, getting involved with one boy and then another and making many lifelong friends. It was a community of young people with compatible ideas. It made getting through our teen years a less turbulent experience than it might have been otherwise. Zionism was instilled in us as well as progressive political issues. I didn't think much of Judaism. That only came years later.

The most important result of my being in Hashomer was my aliyah to Israel, not with a garin and not to kibbutz. In 1967 I was in Berkeley going to the university. I went to Hillel with my Jewish friends where I folk danced weekly and I participated in anti-Vietnam protests with my leftist friends (primarily Jewish) in Students for a Democratic Society (SDS). The Six Day War broke out in June 1967 and at first all of the leftists were very pro-Israel and everyone was frightened about what would happen next. But after Israel was victorious, the SDS folks changed their tune and suddenly there were anti-Israel slogans chalked on sidewalks and walls. At this point I decided to leave the university and make aliyah. I was disenchanted and it was only many years later that I realized that the left was often anti-Israel.

I found Israel to be a very diverse community. My first experience was at Arad learning Hebrew on an ulpan for young people planning to go to Israeli universities. There were folks from all over the world: South America, South Africa, Britain, France, North American, and Australia. I became close friends with the South American group. Arad was in the desert between Beer Sheva and Masada. You can, and I did, walk through the desert to the western side of Masada. Walking through the desert was a spiritual experience like no other. In Arad strong winds would blow at night and herds of camels would pass during the day.

I settled in Jerusalem in an old Arab house in Ohel Shlomo close to the outdoor markets in Machane Yehudah. I started to study at the Hebrew University in the Art History Department. I eventually met Aryeh, who also was studying there in the Sociology Department. It didn't take long until we married on February 9,

1971 accompanied by a bluegrass band of Hashomer folks I had known on seminar in 1964, Zoe and Mimi and Mencher. They made our wedding quite unique, memorable and wonderful. We only had a band because Aryeh's orthodox uncle insisted that we have live music at our wedding. He hadn't planned on blue grass. Aryeh had been raised in an orthodox Jewish home and had attended religious day schools. But he came to Israel in hopes of being able to be a Jew without religion. I was becoming more curious about the Jewish religion on the other hand. It was hard to avoid religion living in Jerusalem, the center of Christianity, Islam and Judaism. And it was hard to avoid religion, as much as we tried, being married into Aryeh's family.

Wishing to escape from Jerusalem on the holiest day of the year when the city was closed down, on Yom Kippur in 1973, Aryeh and I, and our six month old son Yaniv, with our very good friend Mike Comay, visited Chaviva, her six year old daughter Chinanit, and her new husband, Mo, on Kibbutz Barkai. We were in the cotton fields on a gorgeous autumn day when war broke out on the Golan. We felt safe on the kibbutz where everything was very organized. After sleeping in our clothes in a room with blacked out windows ready to get up and go to bomb shelters if we had to, we had to prepare to go back to Jerusalem in the morning. Living through a war, not knowing what to expect was terrifying. After this I decided to fast on Yom Kippur.

Another new experience for me was to instantly become kosher when my in-laws visited us. I invariably made mistakes such as using the meat spoon for the dog's food which wasn't kosher. I only learned about kashrut when I was at Berkeley visiting two friends who suddenly became hysterical because they had put meat in a dairy pot. They had to call one of their parents, a rabbi, to find out what to do. Hashomer did not prepare me for this.

In 1975 we left Jerusalem to live in the development town of Maalot-Tarshikha where Aryeh began to work for Save the Children on programs for the Jewish, Islamic, Christian, and Druze communities in the Western Galilee. While we lived there our sons, Ilan and Moshe, were born. We lived for five years in this small community of 4,000 inhabitants mainly from Morocco. They observed Judaism with a Sephardi twist. We learned about the custom of celebrating Mimouna after Passover and barbecues and belly dancing. People in Maalot were very warm and joyous. It enriched our lives living with them. We lived our lives like secular Israelis even though we lived in a traditional community so that during Passover we would venture down to Akko to buy pitot for the week. I always preferred the Sephardi way of observing the Jewish rituals. During Passover they didn't eat bread but they didn't cut out all the foods that the Ashkenazim did. But things were changing in our lives. We had children in nursery school and in elementary school. They learned all about the Jewish holidays which were a part of Israeli life. Maalot was a small town. Shabbat and the holidays were part of the life cycle of the town and they became a part of ours. Friday we beat the rugs and washed our tile floors getting ready for Shabbat. On Independence Day our kids wore blue and white. We baked hamantaschen and made costumes for our kids on Purim. Chanukah was full of parties in school and friends' houses with enough sufganiot (doughnuts) to give the whole family tummy aches. The country didn't function during the chagim (holidays) of Rosh Hashana, Yom Kippur and Succot and Passover too when folks got into a frenzy of cleaning that I never could comprehend. So suddenly we were knowledgeable about all the holidays. All was good as long as we were in Israel.

Aryeh's religious family in Israel, uncle and aunt and many cousins who became our surrogate parents while living in Israel, were a big part of our life. I experienced my first real Passover seder at their house. It was long and all in Hebrew. Everything was so foreign to me. But through the years it became more and more familiar. Soon I looked forward to Passover seders but never to its preparation. I was becoming knowledgeable about Ashkenazi orthodox rituals and customs. Thankfully, there was little friction between Aryeh's religious family and me even though my background was very different. It was probably because they were very loving and caring. They also accepted our lifestyle.

In 1980 we left Israel. We decided we needed to be closer to our families and further from the terrorist attacks and wars plaguing Israel. We had been in bomb shelters when Israel went into Lebanon and there were several terrorist attacks on our town. Aryeh also wanted to continue his studies.

Our Jewish identity changed radically upon arrival in Philadelphia, living close to my religious in-laws and cousins my kids' age. Almost immediately we enrolled our sons in Jewish Day School and almost just as fast we became permanently kosher. We spent years attending the synagogue where Aryeh's family went which was traditional, meaning orthodox, except men and women sat together. Although I didn't embrace religion, I did get accustomed to it. We now fasted as an extended family on Yom Kippur and had big family meals for all the holidays. We went to synagogue together. We walked to the nearby stream for tashlich together. The boys all learned to read Torah from Aryeh's father and my three sons and their three cousins would alternate reading the portions on Shabbat. And so another community was formed. However, I never got used to the obsessive Ashkenazi preparations for Passover. I yearned to be Sephardi.

My sons grew up. Aryeh worked in Jewish Social Services in Philadelphia. I worked at universities in administration and kept exploring new techniques in art, got a graduate degree at Penn. Life was peaceful.

My sons married and had children. My youngest son, Moshe, settled in Pittsburgh 300 miles from Philadelphia. We moved to Pittsburgh also, a lovely small city with trees and parks and friendly people. We joined various synagogues through the years. Aryeh's parents moved to Pittsburgh too. We would join them for Shabbat in a Chabad congregation for the independent living complex where they lived. The men and women sitting separately. Strangely, I liked sitting just with the women. It was a community. After Aryeh's parents passed away we sought out different synagogues and settled on Tree of Life which was located about five blocks from our home. Rabbis came and went and we were finally more or less settled with Rabbi Meyers who had just relocated from New Jersey. It was October 27, 2018 and it was Aryeh's grandfather's yahrzeit. My grandkids had slept over so I was staying home with them. Aryeh walked to synagogue but not too fast. He was half a block from the synagogue when he saw police cars and heard shooting. Voices were shouting "live shooter, keep away!" Our sense of peace and safety was shattered. The Pittsburgh community of Blacks, Christians, Moslems and Jews were strong in their support and outrage in the murder of eleven congregants. The violence we thought we had escaped found us not only in our town but in the very synagogue we called home. A younger me would have packed her bags and gone back to Israel.

My friend Dvora, who I met at my first moshava when I was twelve, told me that when you begin to write you don't know where you will wind up. She was right. I didn't expect to end at this point. I would like to end with this last year which we spent in lock down. What did I do? Who did I turn to?

It's the year of the Zoom meetings. Every week I meet with my two sisters, one living in Woodland, California and the other in Seattle, Washington. We have never been in such continuous contact. Once a month, I meet with four friends from Hashomer, three living in California, Dvora in Spain and myself in Pittsburgh. We also have never been in such close contact with each other. I zoom with three college friends once a month scattered across the country bringing us closer than ever. The same can be said about the weekly zooms with my three sons. I take art classes on-line learning skills that somehow passed me by while concentrating on abstract acrylic paintings the last number of years. I also zoom with my artist group. We do zoom synagogue services rather irregularly. We do zoom dinners with Pittsburgh friends.

Hashomer gave me a feeling of community and safety and prepared me for a journey. My Jewish journey took me far from the socialist Zionist teachings. Truthfully I have yet to find the perfect spiritual home. But I have found other communities, communities of artists and of people I feel comfortable with as in my youth. I have learned to live with people who have different backgrounds than I have and learned to appreciate the differences. In this year of lock down I sought out these same people that have supported me through the years, starting with Hashomer.

Before I finish, I have to write a note about Andi Fischhoff. What a happy and unexpected coincidence for two shomerniks from opposite sides of the country to find each other in Pittsburgh.

It was such a joy to be able to discuss our background together without having to go into lengthy explanations. Zionism? Kibbutz? Thank you Andi.

Shellie Sherman in a corn field on the chava and with other shomrot

Painting by Shellie Sherman

Shuli Dubinsky now Andersen. From Jackson Heights to Silkeborg, Denmark

I was born in Manhattan in 1947. My parents, Holocaust refugees from Belgium, were living with a distant relative in a one room apartment until I was about three months old. We then moved to Jackson Heights, Queens, where we lived until we made aliya in 1965. The house we lived in was owned by the parents of a childhood friend of my father's, whose sister rescued him from a camp. They were my only Jewish contact and we always spent seder with them. The neighborhood was Irish / Italian Catholic and things were fine until all we kids began school. They went to parochial school and I to PS 148. A few days after school began I was told that they would no longer play with me since I had killed Christ...

Luckily, there were other friends, Jewish, all children of survivors: Browars, Kramans, Warga as well as "natives" like Hillel's parents, others mixed like the Isseroffs. I always knew that my destiny was somehow connected to somewhere called Israel, since my parents had a suitcase packed and ready all through my childhood. In 1958 I went to moshava. A total change in my life!! Other Jews, my age!! Dance and song, friendships, learning some Hebrew and a feeling of belonging, which I had never experienced before. I began to belong to Ken N'Tiv Mordechai, and met other Jews from Queens; Mimi W., Eydie Kaufman, Eric and others. Newtown High School brought Mimi, Eydie, Shimon Kochavi and Gaby Mannheim closer into my life. I was on seminar in 1964-65 on Gal On and Dalya. Many of you on this thread were there too, as well as two people whom I still miss; Ami Isseroff and Shira (Carol Wexler) Z"L. I was no longer in doubt of my Judaism or that I would live in Israel.

I married an Israeli, son of my kibbutz family in Dalya, and we had two sons. Our oldest still lives there with his German wife and their 4 children. The marriage lasted 6 years. I remained on Dalya, commuting to Tel Aviv for two years studying dental hygiene and then worked on the kibbutz. I left Israel in 1980 for Denmark, after having met my husband on a trip here. Both boys remained on Dalya with their father. To make a long story short, the situation between my two sons has made me "lose my religion." My youngest lives today on Or HaGanuz, an ultra-orthodox community near Safat. My sons have not had contact with each other for 25 years.......Their individual interpretation of Judaism has created a schism between them that I cannot accept although I cannot do anything about it. Visits with one family or the other were always like walking through a minefield, careful never to mention "the others". I now have nine grandchildren and a great grandchild whom I have yet to meet because of corona. I always believed that family was the most important for us, especially as the daughter of survivors. I never knew my grandparents. Now, all of my grandchildren have never met each other.

Today, my Jewishness seems to be deeply rooted in the past; in H.H., in the time in Israel, in the friendships which still stretch from 1958 to today. I wish I could find those times again, and the feeling of belonging.

Shuli, with the white sweater over her shoulders, and others, listening to Tzvi Body

Shoshana Kochavi aka Susie Browar–living the life in sunny Vegas

My childhood journey with Hashomer Hatzair began because of my Dad. He belonged to Hashomer Hatzair in Zurich, Switzerland just a few short years before WWII. My love for all things Israel was because of him while my Judaism and the expression of a Jewish religion was from growing up surrounded by my cousins and aunts and uncles and their Jewish orthodoxy. So, my Dad was known as the Shabbos "goy" who could turn on and off the lights on Shabbat while we were left to figure it all out on our own. By high school, I did. It was the year we were taught that there existed more than just the Judao-Christian God. I asked myself, what made my religion have the one true god (aka the chosen people), and not anybody else's? It was then that I decided I was definitely an agnostic and more likely an atheist. In practical terms that meant I could keep all the fun parts of our Jewishness such as holidays and family rituals and ignore the rest! Besides, in HH we had 'our ten commandments' so I was good to go. And go I did.

At age 17, I made aliyah with my family leaving behind both my teenage friends and Hashomer Hatzair. I could say that Hashomer Hatzair gave me my Jewish culture and more importantly taught me about kibbutz. I remember well all the stories of Chana Senesh and Yad Mordecai, all the Israeli singing and dancing, campfires, and moshava and yet for me it was just a means to an end. And that end wasn't so much kibbutz as it was aliyah! I did call Kibbutz Galon, my home while I was in nursing school, but that faded once Shimon and I got married.

Shimon and I remained in Israel (and had three kids), but my parents – we called them the Jewish Bedouins. They made aliyah a few times during those years until they finally ended up back in the States, only for my Mom to go back to Israel after my Dad died.

Somehow through all of their travels they also managed to keep up relationships with quite a few shomrim. (more so than we did). I think many Shomrim came to spend time with my parents because they enjoyed having conversations with my Dad and laughing at my Mom's self-deprecating humor. In Israel my parents were their home away from home. Meanwhile, after 13 years in Israel, Shimon and I came back to the States and two years after that my Mom moved back to Israel. She continued to be the one-stop-shop for many shomrim when they made their way into Tel Aviv.

The cat collage (titled The Kats came a Courtin') was cut out over many of my visits to Israel as I sat with her at the Alzheimer's Center at Tel HaShomer. She loved cats and had left behind the many stray cats she took care of when she finally had to be placed in the Alzheimer's Center. She died almost two years ago at the age of 93.
 Susie

Susie and Elana Tucker

Quilt by Susie Browar and her mom, Evelyn Browar

Stuie Brier

I attend a church service, now via Zoom, regularly. Does that mean I don't have a relationship with, and was not influenced by Jewish heritage? I think not.

What did that influence entail? Well, for one, my parents. They did not observe traditions and weren't religious, but they had a strong sense of being Jewish. My father came here from a shtetl in Poland with his family when he was thirteen. My mother grew up in NYC. Her parents were Romanian. My neighborhood in Bayside, Queens was almost all Jewish, although few traditions were observed by neighbors and friends I knew.

However, many kids went to Hebrew school to prepare for bat and bar mitzvah. My parents came close to not sending me to Hebrew school but then decided it would be good for me to know something about the traditions. So I went to Hebrew school, and I would say it was an important influence. I believed there is a God, and I liked feeling that I was a part of Jewish peoplehood, with its history, customs and ceremonies. I was disturbed, though, that we were taught that God was really angry at us when we didn't observe the commandments of the Torah. One of my teachers told us that if we didn't observe all the mitzvot it was as if we had observed none. Still, I had a positive enough attitude to frequently attend junior congregation Shabbat services after my bar mitzvah.

Theo brought me into Hashomer Hatzair. The emphasis on Jewish peoplehood and self-determination appealed to me. I thought some Zionist ideas provided an analysis of Jewish social location and history that made sense, although I didn't believe Israel could be the homeland of all Jews. I appreciated the emphasis on socialist ideals and concern for the oppressed. I enjoyed being with the people in the t'nua and had many fun times at Moshava and at activities of "G'dud Ataza" at the Queens Ken.

I continued attending Shabbat services at my neighborhood synagogue while in Hashomer. I don't recall mentioning that to anyone but I told some people in the movement I believed in God.

I did talk about the t'nua to people at the Shabbat services. The youth leaders at the service were against its secularism but asked me to give a talk about the movement. I gave the talk, although I was surprised to be asked. I think they appreciated the commitment of movement folks to the Jewish people and Israel but, of course, expressed unhappiness that there was no role for Torah in H. H.

In 1965 I went on seminar and on Rosh Hashana of that year, I and two other people walked from Kibbutz Mishmar HaEmek to a neighboring religious Moshav and attended their service. The shaliach from the kibbutz was very unhappy when he found out. He called a meeting of all of us on seminar and said that it made no sense to attend a service like that if we weren't committed to Halacha. He said he respected orthodox religious folks in Israel because they really practiced. But just to attend services at Rosh Hashana or every now and then was a kind of hypocrisy.

I was upset and got up and left the meeting. However, much later, thinking about it, I thought I saw his point. Although I had a feel for worship, I knew I wasn't going to observe dietary laws and festival customs. After seminar, I stopped attending Shabbat services. I hadn't planned to make aliyah, and after many people did, I no longer had a Jewish community.

In the years that followed, I avidly read books on Zen and other Eastern traditions by Alan Watts. Interestingly, he wrote in an essay that if you understood God via Jewish or Christian traditions, you would have to engage those understandings or you might have problems doing Zen. Briefly, I went to a zendo weekly for a while and then was involved with a meditation group in a Hindu tradition. Later, I started volunteering at a soup kitchen in Park Slope, Brooklyn and met a number of progressive Catholics and Christians of other denominations. They believed in Jesus, and that he had manifested God by especially reaching out to the poor, the needy, the marginalized and neglected. He touched lives of some outside the Jewish fold. He dined with religious outcasts, which had meaning to me as an LGBTQ person. He taught that the Shabbat was meant for people and not the other way around and that laws weren't the ultimate thing. The movement around Jesus originated in the Jewish community of his day. Later in history, churches persecuted Jews and many others in the name of God but many church people today are taking a hard, critical look at this. Christian nationalism and conservative fundamentalism needn't be the only way to interpret and relate to this tradition.

My meditation group had taught that certain masters could be divine manifestations, and Jesus was one. Watts believed that Jesus had had a very profound experience of "cosmic consciousness". I accepted in faith that Jesus was and is the God I had always believed in, in person, and would be in our corner despite defects and ways lives can go wrong. I eventually became a member of the Episcopal Church.

Stuie

Margie and Stuie

Talya Rubin – Carol Shama

I was born in Brooklyn, the middle child of three. My parents identified strongly as Jews but went to synagogue only on the High Holidays. Mostly, Judaism was about celebrating a few holidays with a lot of food. My mother sent me to a Talmud Torah four days a week after school where I learned biblical Hebrew. It was an orthodox synagogue so my Jewish education ended when I was 12. When I was 14 I attended Camp Ramah, a conservative Jewish summer camp. I hated it. Way too much praying especially on Shabbat. The next year when I refused to go back, my mother came across an ad in the New York Times for a Jewish summer camp named Shomria. She had absolutely no idea what type of camp it was but from her point of view any camp, especially a Jewish one, would be better than dealing with me in the city for the summer.

I immediately loved Camp Shomria. I liked everything about it. The camping, the dancing, the freedom, the ideology. I had never met such wonderful, interesting and idealistic people. That first summer I dreamed of the day I would earn my chultzah. The more involved I became in the movement, and I did become very involved, the more my mother panicked. Her greatest fear was that I would leave her and make aliyah. I was perplexed by her resistance to my involvement in Hashomer Hatzair because she had always given me the impression that she loved Israel and in my mind making aliyah would be the highest expression of that love. So in spite of her very strong objections, I went to Israel for six months to Kibbutz Galon and to Kibbutz Mishmar Ha-emek. Sadly for my future as a Zionist, I was very unhappy during those six months. I gained about 30 pounds and upon returning home I cut all ties to the movement.

So what have I done with the rest of life? I was the director of a food cooperative in Buffalo, New York. I ran recreational programs for adults with developmental disabilities for about 15 years. I was a teen services librarian and then the director of a library in a small city in upstate New York. I did the latter job for over 20 years until I retired at 68. I married a man who was not Jewish but who became a Jew by choice about 30 years into our marriage. We had two children and have five grandchildren. My son is the co-president of his tiny synagogue in Geneva, NY and my daughter lives in Salt Lake City and sends her children to a Jewish day school. Both have visited Israel and enjoyed their time there but neither was bitten by the Zionist bug.

About 20 years ago I visited Israel with my brother. During that visit I learned about Shomer-net and I reconnected with Bonnie Ellinger. What a wonderful reunion that was! Thanks to her I came to the reunion that was held at the High Line in Manhattan. That was probably one of the most unique experiences of my entire life. With the exception of Bonnie, who I had seen in New York and in Israel a few times after I had left HH, the last time I had seen any of the folks who attended that reunion I had been in my late teens and so had they. I cannot begin to describe how stunned I was to see that we had all done some serious aging!

My years in Hashomer Hatzair were some of the happiest and most intense years in my life. I am grateful to Margie Ben Dov for reaching out to me. I look forward to reading all of your entries in the book and learning where your lives have taken you.

Tzippy Kleiner

I was born in Jerusalem to a Hasidic family. My connection to Judaism was through the words of the prophets and not through stories about the "Conquest of the Land" (Book of Joshua). So my connection to Hashomer Hatzair seems to me most natural and fits the world view in which I grew up.

The United States was not a place where I felt at home. I had lived as a child in an independent Israel in the late 1940s and the early 1950s, and this made me sensitive to any kind of Jewish segregation or the labeling of Judaism as a separate minority and community. It was clear to me that my place was in Israel, and I knew that through the movement I would find a safe way back to Israel. I also connected to the idea of the kibbutz and the community and sharing, that for me was a continuation of the religion I had grown up on.

My activity in the movement as madricha filled me with happiness and enthusiasm and, in general, I also found an ideological home.

On my transition from my Hasidic home to Hashomer Hatzair, there was also a Bnei Akiva stopover. Before the Occupation Bnei Akiva's ideology was similar to that of HH. Before we moved to New York my family lived in London and I joined Bnei Akiva there. I also hung around with members of Hashomer Hatzair whose ideology didn't seem that much different from that of Bnei Akiva. They were just more friendly and accepting!!!!

One of the first things I did in New York was look for Hashomer Hatzair. When I arrived at the lishka I was greeted by the shaliach, Hilik Harari, and within two weeks I found myself being sent to a Passover camp in Detroit as cultural support. I used to say that life gives us gifts that we do not always immediately recognize. Living in New York in the late fifties and early sixties, the high school I attended, and my involvement in the movement, were the things that shaped me and they form the foundation of the tapestry which encompasses my life story. And, of course, those turbulent years in New York had an impact on my world view and way of life.

I also met Murray, my husband, in the movement. Together we created the Kleiner family. Essential members of our family are those same members of the movement that have been with us all the way to this day. And some of these connections have continued on down through the second generation.

I was exposed as a child to a humane and accepting Judaism. It was a Judaism that was very different from what is found today in religious politics. In the Judaism of my childhood, they talked about the sanctity of man.
So my ideology hasn't changed, only the setting.

I was the only one in my family to return to Israel. My siblings were all able to adjust to life in the United States.

Murray was born in a refugee camp in Germany in 1946 to Holocaust survivor parents. His father Zelig was a Bundist from Wolbrom, a small town near Krakow, in Poland. Born into an ultra-Orthodox family he rebelled and became non-religious. His mother Judy, came from a wealthy Warsaw family. The couple met at the end of the war. Unfortunately, we were never told how they met and we never asked.

Murray, Mencher, Lewis and Yechiel were in the same grade at Stuyvesant High School, and were also in the same kvutza in the movement. Mencher introduced me to Murray at the high school Hillel Club where I was asked to teach Israeli folk dancing. He also invited Murray to come to Mosh Horef. And that's where Murray and I became a couple.

After my training on the chava I immigrated to Kibbutz Barkai. Murray joined me there eight months later, in the spring of 1965. Murray and I got married. A year later, in the fall, our eldest, Mira, was born.

We were adopted by the Shagrin family on Barkai and we became a close part of their family. My connection with the Shagrin family is strong and important to me to this day. We left Barkai after five years so that Murray could continue his studies in Jerusalem, but our connection with Barkai exists to this day. Murray is buried there, and I have a plot nearby.

Our story began to be woven into a tapestry with threads and motifs, that in some way, all have their source in Hashomer Hatzair.

In Jerusalem, where we moved in 1969, a group of friends was formed that included Zoie and Mimi, Zvi and Judy Body, Lewie and Dalia, Ariela, Mencher, Baruch and Andi, Zvi Brazil and Meri, Margie, and Yechiel, and Murray's sister Susan and Zoie's sister Pnina. They were all students in Jerusalem. This was a wonderful basis for a group that still is with me today. Some of that group became an integral part of our family with all that it entails. Noa Mencher, as a nurse, together with our sons Ariel and Yoav, helped us in Murray's last moments. We have never lost our connection with Lewie's family. The kvutza that I was the madricha of in the Queens ken is still connected: Dottee, Mimi, Shuli, Ariela, and Eydie. They are still friends, and they are also my friends. The distance between us that existed then, is no longer relevant.

When I moved from Jerusalem to Karkur to be near my family, I didn't come to a social desert. Dalia Meidan, who was in my kvutza in the ken in Los Angeles, Yonina Rabinov who was Murray's madricha, and Ariela, all live in Pardes Hana-Karkur.

To sum up: At the age of 13 I joined Hashomer Hatzair in London. At the age of 15 I came to the lishka in New York. Since then we have woven together a rich and diverse tapestry filled with colors and threads that are strong and everlasting.

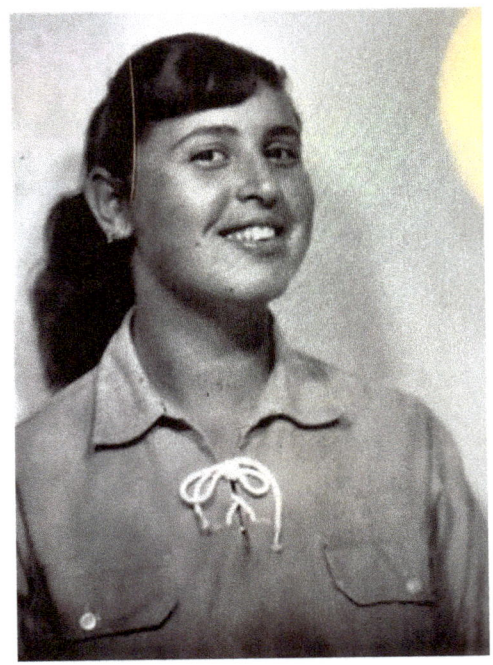

Uri's Reflections – Uri Treisman

Much of my childhood was shaped by my father's schizophrenia, my mom's struggle to support us when my dad was institutionalized in a state hospital and my often debilitating shyness. My mom grew up in the Hebrew Orphans Asylum in Manhattan and left it with no fondness for religion or any form of Jewish practice, but still cared about her Jewish cultural identity. Her mom died when she was two years old and her father was some variety of psychotic, which is why she grew up in the "home" as the Asylum was called. He was orthodox and survived by telling people's fortunes in Jewish old age homes. Our apartment house neighbors were a mix of Holocaust survivors, both Jews and Catholics, and of secular Jews doing their best to protect their children from knowledge of the horrors that their neighbors had experienced.

My zayde insisted I attend a yeshiva after public school which I did from the first grade until the week he died a few months after my tenth birthday. I loved the yeshiva certainly for the attention I received and for the stories and the study routines. In retrospect, yeshiva was a much needed escape from my reality. My mother hated it and wanted me to learn to deal with the real world. When my zayde died, she got me a job with Louie, the neighborhood butcher, who was a Labor Zionist. We were on welfare and needed the few dollars I could earn. He introduced me to Zionism and to Dror. My mother did send me to the Flatbush Jewish Center for Bar Mitzvah lessons. It was a joke. Socialist Zionism became my religion. My dad came home for a few months when I was in the 6th grade which was a nightmare. I escaped into Dror and into books on Jewish history, Marxism and, in the eighth grade, mathematics – as far away from my surroundings as I could get.

In the seventh grade I started going to Washington Square Park on Sundays for the folk music and with the hope against hope that maybe I could find a girlfriend. On one of those Sundays, I, shy, awkward Uri, saw two girls whose beauty literally took my breath away. Somehow, I managed to approach them. Turned out they were not only beautiful, but razor sharp and funny. Yep, Nechama and Shira. They invited me to the Bronx ken and I was hooked. So much for my loyalty to Dror. Shira and I were a couple through much of our high school years. Although after 50 + years, I am ready to admit, it was really Nechama I was interested in although her sister Batya was also in my peripheral line of sight and a close second in my active fantasy life.

Hashomer Hatzair gave me the chance to reinvent myself. It wasn't easy but the commitment to aliya meant I didn't have to worry about my future self so I could put all my energy into trying to reconstruct my then current self. It was a confusing time.

In the Bronx ken, I came to be accepted as a member in good standing. I learned a lot about leadership and about teaching. Indeed, if you look at the programs that were the basis of my MacArthur Fellowship, I have no doubt you'll see their roots in Ken Hachoresh and Ken Nirim in Los Angeles.

Events, of course, can change a life's direction and the viper bite on Dalya certainly changed mine. I had petit mal seizures for some time and wasn't able to drive until my mid-30s. I fell in love with Dvora, we married, decided kibbutz was out, moved first to Brandeis and then to Berkeley for grad school. We were secular Jews without much of a community. I found grad school really difficult. It took me 14 years to finish my dissertation and by year three or four grad school killed our marriage. We remain very close friends. We recently celebrated our 50th wedding anniversary (and the 40th of our divorce) on the Costa Brava where she has lived for many years.

Single for a few years and needing a community, I went to Israeli folk dancing on a lark and entered into a five-year relationship with one of the SF Bay Area's leading Israeli folk dance teachers. That connected me to various Jewish Community Centers, and I immersed myself in Jewish cultural life and volunteerism and community service. In 1991, I was offered a wonderful professorship at UT Austin and definitely found myself a stranger in a very strange world. I felt more distant from Texas Jews than from Ethiopian Jews.

As part of my hiring package, Governor Ann Richards offered me a position on the newly forming TX Governor's Commission on Volunteerism and Community Service. And soon after, I was asked to lead the process of developing the State's math and science school curriculum. Thus, I was on the road every week in community meetings, in churches, sometimes honoring local volunteers, and other times meeting with very conservative fundamentalist school board members.

It was eye-opening and definitely other-worldly. We've all read myriad accounts of Jews encountering antisemitism, both biographical and fictional, but now I came to understand those accounts in a radically different way. On one of my first "official" trips to rural Texas, a mayor asked me, "What do the Jews think about ...." I was invited to meet with a church study group. I prepared diligently for the first such meeting which I assumed would be about evolution. It turned out the lay minister was a dentist who knew all about viral evolution. They had never met a Jew and wanted to know how to say something in Biblical Hebrew. Two of their local teachers disagreed – neither being correct as it turned out. They treated me with extraordinary respect which taught me that for them, Jews had nothing to do with actual living Jews like us. It wasn't until I began working with legislators that I met a few rabid anti-Semites, although they were quickly decreasing in number, according to two Jews I knew in the Texas House.

And then, of course, there is the antisemitism among more than a few in the Black and Latin communities where I do considerable work. It has very different sources in these communities. There are days when my Jewish identity feels shaped more by non-Jews than Jews. Whatever its sources, with the movement probably being the most important, I wear my evolving Jewishness on my name tag: I've kept Uri as my name.

If we should have more meetings, which I hope will be the case, I'll tell you the story of my attempt as a representative of the Governor's office to get local Church of Christ and Baptist leaders to come together to address the extraordinarily high teenage pregnancy rate in their Bible Belt town's high school. Then there was a time when a House member, who referred to me as a person of the Mosaic persuasion, asked in one of those rare moments when we agreed on a policy matter, if I had had a Paul of Tarsis epiphany. I calmly explained in open session that Jews didn't have epiphanies, we had circumcisions. And soto voce, followed that with a variant of the old Jewish joke – to have an epiphany , I'd have to sew my foreskin back on. But not to worry, my mother saves everything. I wasn't as quiet as I thought and a Jewish House member seated behind me interrupted with "Point of order, point of order, did the gentleman from The University of Texas actually say...."

Today, I study Jewish history, culture and literature with a wonderful group of friends. I mentor Jewish students as well as others, and no longer feel like a stranger in a strange world. I know I've been extraordinarily lucky, professionally and personally – a 20 year wonderful marriage to Linda Chaput. Hashomer Hatzair was a powerful shaping force in my life and I am so happy to reconnect with all of you.
Chazak v'Ematz
– uri

I Was Born a Jewish Refugee – Yehuda Reisman

I was born a refugee in Poland after WWII, to a Romanian mother and a Polish father who, separately, ran away from the Nazis into the Soviet Union. They met, married, and conceived me in Kazakhstan near the Chinese border. They returned to Poland after the war and there I was born. At my Bris, I was named Yehuda Leib Reisman after my grandfather who had been murdered by Nazis together with their Polish collaborators. Lewis became my official name in the fourth grade because of my embarrassment when my teachers could not manage to pronounce Yehuda.

When I was five weeks old, my parents escaped Poland with the aid of the Zionist Bricha organization and moved to a refugee camp in West Germany. When I was four, we moved to Brooklyn, where I lived between the ages of four and 21.

As a child, I was surrounded by Holocaust survivors, each with stories of suffering and survival amid death. We were a nuclear family with no grandparents and no uncles or aunts, most of whom were dead, and a few of whom were alive in the distant Soviet Union, Romania, and Israel. Yiddish was my first language, and the language of our home and of my parents' friends. From my earliest memories, I was a Jew and a refugee and did not identify as an American. I remember hating the Christmas season. It was presented on all the media as a holiday of good will which included everyone, everyone except me that is.

My father attended a small Chasidic shteible (prayer room) and, occasionally, he took me to the Lubavicher synagogue and community center on Eastern Parkway in Brooklyn, for the holidays, especially Simchat Torah and Purim.

There were times when I yearned to be one of the Chasidim. They had a group ethos of mutual support. No one belonging to a Chasidic group went homeless or hungry. They found employment for their own or helped them go into business. They helped find brides and grooms for those who needed help. They visited the sick, helped celebrate marriages and births, and helped bury their dead.

Soon after my Bar Mitzva, I began to have severe doubts about the existence of God. These doubts generally focused on the Holocaust. My question was, and remains: How could an All-Knowing and All-Seeing, but merciful God, who regularly intervenes in human affairs, allow six million innocent people to be tortured to death. With my loss of faith as a teenager, I had an identity crisis.

If I didn't believe in God and didn't practice my religion, was I, in fact, still Jewish? This problem was solved for me by joining Hashomer Hatzair and becoming a Zionist.

Moving to live in Israel, learning to speak and read the Hebrew language, becoming an Israeli citizen, and serving in the Israeli army, all became my way of expressing my Jewish identity. In Israel, I met many people very much like me and felt very much at home.

In 1976, I moved back to NY, mostly for better medical training. I came back with an Israeli wife and a baby daughter and life was good. We had two more children and my career was successful. I thought about going back to Israel, but my wife was against it and it seemed economically risky with a growing family to support. We found ourselves, like other immigrants, faced with the impossible task of trying to transfer a foreign culture to our American raised children.

In 2014, after 38 years in the US, Dalia and I moved back to Israel. My career was essentially finished, and my kids were economically established. My main regret is that my children and grandchildren are distant from me, both geographically and culturally.

For better or worse, Hashomer Hatzair has affected my whole life. Through the movement, I flew to Israel as a volunteer during the Six Day War. While working on Kibbutz Barkai that summer I applied to Hadassah Medical School. While studying at Hadassah, I met my wife, the Head Nurse of Pediatrics at the time.

I love living in Jerusalem, a unique city, with a spirituality that I have not felt anywhere else. I feel myself Israeli in a way that I was never American. I read Hebrew novels, go to Hebrew theater and Hebrew cinema. I study the Tanach, the ancient book written by Jews and adopted by the whole world. Like every other country in the world, there is good and bad here. This is my country, and I will fight to make it a better, more just place.

Although I am a Jewish/Israeli nationalist, I no longer identify as a Zionist. Zionism was always a term more useful for those remaining abroad, rather than for those living in Israel. My father used to repeat an old Jewish witticism: "A Zionist is a Jew who gives money so that a second Jew will convince a third Jew to move to Israel." Israel needs to become a normal country where the government is responsive to all of its citizens, Jewish or not, rather than being responsive to the foreign Jews who are not citizens, have no stake in the country, and rarely have a good grasp as to what is going on here.

Yehuda

Yehuda and Dalia's wedding in Jerusalem. Present are: Yona, Dov, Zoie, Tzippy, Meri, Mimi, Pnina, Lilit, Baruch, Nurit S, Murray and Susie K

Yolande Bonan Gottdiener - Montreal/Kibbutz Galon

Okay, here goes for someone not used to writing but somehow, I think this is going to be long.

I joined the movement when my basketball partner, Chana (Anna) Fuerstenberg asked me to come to the "ken" that Friday night. She was insistent and two years later I came to the ken not knowing what to expect. It turned out to be a sicha on Borochov that night. Not understanding a thing – I did not come from a socialist, communist, intellectual or informed background – I struggled to understand what this upside down triangle and our lives meant. BUT, there was dancing – Israeli folk, dancing at the end. Everyone together – no matter what age – and it felt great. I was at home – not in a club house or anything like that and I fell in love with HH.

I came from a Sephardic Egyptian-Lebanese observant family. My father put tfilin on until his last day. He went to the synagogue, a big Ashkenazi one which allowed us Sephardic immigrants a room in the basement to pray. There were enough men to form a minyan but hardly more. We, as children, on Saturdays would join our fathers (no room for women) and mostly play outside. Since there was a "girls meeting" Saturdays after prayers, my father allowed me to join them. "Mesibos Shabbos" – turned out it was a Lubavitch girls club. But what I knew was that I did not feel as "religious" as them and in the end my sister and I stopped going.

I had a hard time staying in HH. My parents could never afford to send me to summer camps and I worked in the summers since I was 13. Even when I became a madricha I could not go to Shomria. But I was persistent and one year they allowed me to go for three weeks after the shaliach gave my parents a huge discount.

In 1966 I managed, with some of the money I earned that summer and a huge discount from the Sochnout, to go on Machon Le'Madrichei Chul and the rest is history.

In Israel, at the end of that training year, the Six Day War broke out. I was on Revadim and visited my chaverim who had made aliya during that war ; Elana Barskey (who was my madricha), Dov Gottdiener who I later married, and Yona and Marty who lived on kibbutz already.

I made aliya in April 1969, after a horrible time at the Hachshara, and I have been on Galon since.

Yonina Rabinov – other names: Yonina Frankel, Jo Ann Frankel Sperber Rabinov

I was literally born into Hashomer Hatzair so that was the main influence on my identity, both as a Jew and Zionist, and on my social and political outlook.

My parents met in the movement at the end of the 1930s, on hachshara while waiting for 'certificates' to make aliyah, and then had their lives turned inside out because of World War II. My youngest years passed in Washington Heights, then too, a typical Jewish New York enclave, then in Flatbush, Brooklyn. My father served in the army and when I was born, October 1944, he was shipped overseas and I only met him when I was about 18 months old. At that point any thoughts of Palestine were mostly theoretical as they sought to build a married life.

My mother's parents were Poalei Zion, and even made aliyah when my mother was six months old, eventually returning to the States because my grandfather could not make a living. But they remained Zionists. My grandfather wrote articles for a New York Hebrew newspaper. They were not observant at all.

My father's parents were orthodox Jews, my grandfather served as Rabbi for his small East New York Brooklyn congregation. However, four of the six children joined Zionist movements, my aunt and uncles making aliyah to kibbutzim in the 30s. So, in the 50s they too made aliyah.

My parents bought a house in Brooklyn with the Isseroffs, Zoie and Pnina's parents, Noam and Laya. So, our house became the fulcrum of that generation's Socialist Zionist organization, called PZL (Progressive Zionist League) then API. My father was the treasurer for HH and the senior organizations from the mid 50s to about 1962. They were part of the failed attempt to create an urban Israeli cooperative in the 1960s along with several of the parents of this group. They made aliyah, in my footsteps in 1963, and eventually ended up as kibbutz members in Kfar Menachem, which was 'kibbutz aliya bet' of HH North America.

I was brought up as a cultural Jew, no worship of any kind. But my parents enrolled me in Bialik School for first and second grades, so there, and at my grandparents', I was exposed to more traditional observances. Third grade and up, I was in regular public school, in a neighborhood where the classes were 95% Jewish. The Catholic kids went to Catholic school, the only antisemitism I encountered was that those kids on our block weren't supposed to play with us.

In 1956 my parents and the Isseroffs made a pilot trip/visit to family in Israel. We lived in Givatayim. I was in seventh grade. It was an eventful year, the Sinai War, I lived in a bet yeladim in Kfar Menachem for two months, I learned Hebrew and got a taste of the real Israel. It was still days of rationing and my mother cooked on a ptiliyah, think camp stove. We were 50 kids in a class! The kids were really good to me, Americans were rare on the ground in those days.

We returned to Brooklyn and I to HH and junior high.

I was a very orthodox HHer. I believed, or at least tried to believe, all I was taught. My yearbook signings are full of 'have a great time in Israel.' For immediately after, in 1961, I was sent to the Machon. I was nearly the youngest there and was fascinated by the variations in Zionist beliefs in our groups. We spent half the year in Jerusalem studying Hebrew, and many other Jewish subjects, to prepare us to return to the USA and lead our organizations before making aliyah. The other half year was in kibbutz, like the seminars most of your group attended. And we of HH were forced to return before the famous Machon European tour, in order to be at Moshava that summer.

I did go to Brooklyn College for a year before marrying my first husband, Norman Sperber, Ami's older brother, and making aliyah. We tried kibbutz for about six months, then bought an apartment in Ramat Aviv, where Tali, my oldest was born. For various reasons we returned to the States after about two years, my boys were born in Princeton. We lived in Kendall Park, NJ. I did my B.Sc in education. Then we decided to make aliya again, both because of the pull of the family and the question of how to raise Jewish children without a synagogue.

In 1972 we made aliya to Kibbutz Barkai, where I remained for 16 years. I was divorced, then remarried. Amnon is a ben kibbutz who joined me in Barkai. I had two more kids, girls who are now in their 40s. The older three in their 50s. All five are married and live in Israel. All three girls live within ten minutes of us. In Barkai, I was an early childhood teacher, then the administrator of the kibbutz primary school and a librarian. I also was the librarian at the high school, Mevo'ot Iron, for two years before leaving the kibbutz.

Leaving the kibbutz at age 44 was a very difficult decision. Our parents all were kibbutz members as were most of our families. However, we landed well in city Israel. Only the girls were still at home. We lived in Haifa. I worked at U. of Haifa Library in various positions, eventually as head of reference. My mother tongue and love of working with words, the computer, helping with research, made it a most rewarding occupation. When Amnon got work as head of maintenance in Ra'anana, we moved to Pardes Hanna, where we live today. I retired some ten years ago.

Upon retirement, I took a course in lampworking, making beads from glass on a torch, and have also returned to jewelry making and so have turned this into a side gig, not particularly lucrative but most satisfying.
(Plug: www.yoninajewelry.etsy.com).

We also love to travel. Israel can be a pressure cooker, and so we try to escape two times a year, mostly to Europe, but also to the USA. Both Amnon and I had plans to fill in the gaps in our Jewish education, Amnon being even less acquainted with traditional Judaism than me, but reality got in our way. Perhaps after the current craziness we will take those courses in the local Golden Age Club. Meanwhile, I rediscovered Israeli folk dancing, and we dance three times a week. We are probably the oldest in some of the venues.

Until recently we had a pull in two directions, visiting Amnon's mother, still alive at 110 and in Shaar Hagolan (she died last month), and our grandkids, who lived nearby and whose parents needed us to fill in the childcare gaps. The kids are older now, so family gatherings happen around Shabbat meals and visits. Both of us are only children, so our kids are our essential family.

I suppose that in many ways my life has had a different trajectory from most of you. I did not join or stay in HH as rebellion. Aliya was to family, not from it. I feel more Israeli than American today, although I follow news and maintain a close relationship with Fran Marton (Ronit Kaplan) and my few remaining American cousins. My close friends here are still those who had a similar HH experience; Ariela Ehrlich, Tzippy Kleiner, Dalya Meidan (Gura) and Mary Ellen Robbins, (Miriam Reinhold) who lives mostly in Zurich. There is something about having had the HH North American experience together that makes having to explain ourselves unnecessary.

Yonina's graduation picture, left
and her kvutza from Ken Masada, Brooklyn taken at Camp Shomria

Glossary of words and phrases

aliya – going to live in Israel, the people who go-oleh(m), olah(f), olim(pl.)

anivot bogrim – scarves worn by older members of the youth movement

Aretz – Israel, **Eretz Israel** – the land of Israel

bayit – house/home

ben/bat kibbutz – a child (m,f) born and raised on a kibbutz

bet knesset – synagogue

bet-shimush – bathroom

Hechalutz – HeChalutz Farm – Chalutz (chalutza) means pioneer, **chava – chavat hachshara** – all refer to the training farm in Hightstown, NJ, that was meant to prepare members of the movement for kibbutz life and that closed about 50 years ago. Recently Dvora Treisman found this on the Internet. Apparently, the chava will be open to tourism. Here is the link. https:// njjewishnews.timesofisrael.com/hightstown-farm-prepared-pioneers-for-aliya/

Chag HaBikurim – Shavuot or Shavuos

chanukiya – a Chanuka menorah

Charedim – ultra-orthodox people

chaver, chavera, chaverim, chevra – member of the movement (male, female, plural) also means friend and chevra is friends or group of friends

chavura or **havurah** – a small group of like-minded Jews who assemble for the purposes of facilitating Shabbat and holiday prayer services, sharing communal experiences such as lifecycle events, or Jewish learning.

cheder – room, literally but cheder was the term for a religious school

cheder-ochel – dining hall in a kibbutz

chug – literally a circle but refers to a study or interest group

chultzot shomriot – blue shirts with white laces worn by members of the movement

chupa – wedding canopy in a traditional Jewish wedding

chutzpa – nerve, as in taking liberties – has become an accepted word in the American lexicon.

drasha – **drashot** – sermon or a teaching, plural

echad mi ha Amerikayim – one of the Americans

falcha – the unirrigated field crops like wheat

gan yeladim – children's house in a kibbutz

glidah – ice cream

halutz, halutza or chalutz (a) – pioneer (male, female)

iton – newsletter

Kabbalat Shabbat – welcoming the Sabbath

kashrut – kosher laws

kehilla – community

ken – literally a bird's nest - a base or place for movement activities, as in "the Bronx ken, Ken HaChoresh" or "the Queens ken, Ken N'tiv Mordechai"

Klezmer (band) – instrumental musical tradition of Ashkenazi Jews of Central and Eastern Europe

kova tembel – a soft hat worn back in the day by many kibbutzniks – literally a dunce cap

kovshim – the younger members of HH

kupah – the structure for holding money in common for a group, also a cash register

kvutza – literally group – the younger kids were grouped in a kvutza according to age and sex at each ken

lishka – office – usually refers to the main office of the movement

lul – a chicken coop

ma pitom? – an Israeli expression with no exact translation but is essentially the equivalent of WTF? About something coming out of left field, out of the blue.

Machon Le'Madrichei Chul – Institute for foreign leaders – madrichim from outside Israel

Mazkir T'nua – secretary of the movement

madrich, madricha – group leader in the movement (male, female)

Mapam – political party associated with the HH kibbutz movement (Kibbutz Artzi)

Mesibos Shabbos – literally, Saturday parties

moadon – a club or meeting room. Most kibbutzim have this kind of space for people to hang out, drink tea or coffee, and read or play board games and, in the old days, the only tv set was there.

mo'adon merkaz – a central gathering of the older HH New York members held in Manhattan maybe once a month or as needed usually for fun

moshava (mosh kayitz) – summer camp, **mosh choref** – winter camp

mossad chinuchi – an educational institution

oleh, olah – see aliyah

peula – an activity

pitot – pocket breads common in the mid-east

pluga – at a certain age (16/17) the groups across the city were organized into a pluga

refet – raftanim – the dairy – the people who work in the dairy

rosh ken, rosh mosh – the director of the ken or the summer camp

shaliach – adult kibbutz member -- and family -- sent by the Israeli kibbutz movement to oversee/support the youth movement in cities in North America (New York, Detroit, Los Angeles, Toronto, Montreal) – an emissary. A **shaliach** or **shlicha** comes on **shlichut.**
shichva – age group

shiksa – a non-Jewish woman

shmira – guard duty

shomer Shabbat – keeper of the Sabbath

shomeret /shomer /shomrim – member of the movement (feminine, male, plural)

sichat kibbutz – the weekly kibbutz discussions in which kibbutz policy is determined by popular vote – a direct democracy
Sochnout – the Jewish Agency

tachat – **tuchus**, backside

tallit – prayer shawl

tfilin – phylacteries – men put these on to pray

tiyul – a hike or tour

t'nua – the movement

Tzahal – Israel Defense Forces

tzrif – a shack – founders lived in them and later new member candidates and volunteers
tzurus – troubles, from Yiddish – in Hebrew it is **tzaarot**

ulpan – intensive Hebrew language instruction program for new immigrants, often residential
vatikim – the veterans (founders) of the kibbutz
yeshiva bochers – orthodox male students at a Hebrew school (a yeshiva)

The seminar on Kibbutz
Mishmar HaEmek, 1966

155

And here is how we look now...

Amira and Steve Suffet

Ariela Ehrlich

Bonnie Ellinger and Paul Golding

Claudia (Chedva) Tublin and family

David Mencher and Family

Donnie Goldstein

Dorothea (Dottee) Dorenz

Dvora Treisman

Joey, David Appel, Elana Tucker,Elana M.
Tzippy Braff, Ira Orenstein - Shomria Reunion

Eydie Tamar Kaufman Levy

Eric Corson

Gaby Mannheim and wife

Guy Koretz and family

Joan (Nechama) Price/Rahav

Joey & Miriam
Beinin & family

Laura and Mike MacAlevey

Lenor De Cruz

Laura Lilit Schatzberg and friend in Odessa, Ukraine

Margie Ben Dov

Meri Wallace

Mimi Wolf

Mimi Tanaman

Philip Clement
and grandsons

Shellie Sherman

Shuli Andersen

Susie Browar and Mike Steuer

Carol (Talya) Rubin Shama

אנחנו כאן!

Tzippy Kleiner

Yehuda and Dalia Reisman

Uri Treisman and Linda Chaput

Evelyn Goodman   and her dog Molly

Yonina Frankel
Rabinov

Fran Marton

Artwork by Dorothea Dorenz

www.ingramcontent.com/pod-product-compliance
Lightning Source LLC
Chambersburg PA
CBHW041535120626
46551CB00019B/2712

* 9 7 9 8 9 8 5 4 0 1 4 0 0 *